The Brave

MW01601902

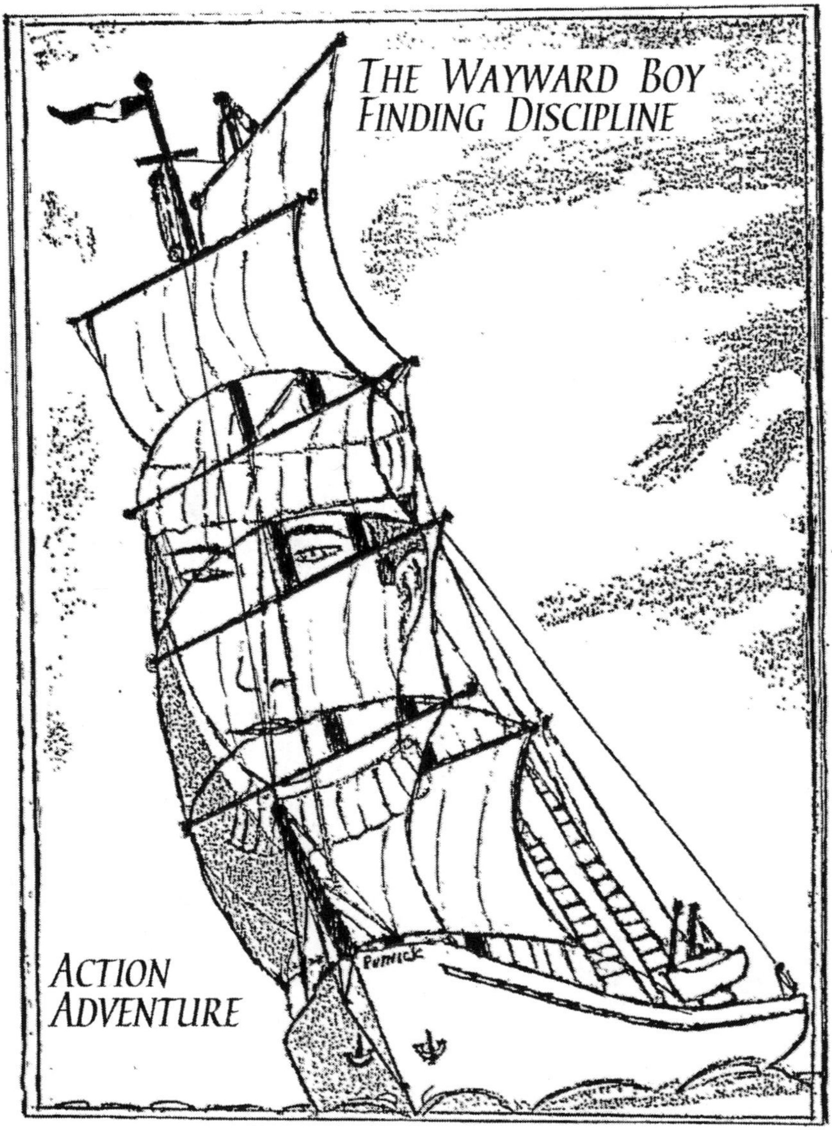

The Wayward Boy
Finding Discipline
Putnick
Action
Adventure

Voyages on the Tall Ship "Putnick"

Note for Librarians: A cataloguing record for this book is available from Library and Archives Canada at www.collectionscanada.ca/amicus/index-e.html
ISBN 1-4120-6508-9

Printed in Victoria, BC, Canada. Printed on paper with minimum 30% recycled fibre. Trafford's print shop runs on "green energy" from solar, wind and other environmentally-friendly power sources.

PUBLISHING™

Offices in Canada, USA, Ireland and UK
This book was published *on-demand* in cooperation with Trafford Publishing. On-demand publishing is a unique process and service of making a book available for retail sale to the public taking advantage of on-demand manufacturing and Internet marketing. On-demand publishing includes promotions, retail sales, manufacturing, order fulfilment, accounting and collecting royalties on behalf of the author.

Book sales for North America and international:
Trafford Publishing, 6E–2333 Government St.,
Victoria, BC V8T 4P4 CANADA
phone 250 383 6864 (toll-free 1 888 232 4444)
fax 250 383 6804; email to orders@trafford.com
Book sales in Europe:
Trafford Publishing (UK) Limited, 9 Park End Street, 2nd Floor
Oxford, UK OX1 1HH UNITED KINGDOM
phone 44 (0)1865 722 113 (local rate 0845 230 9601)
facsimile 44 (0)1865 722 868; info.uk@trafford.com
Order online at:
trafford.com/05-1419

14 13 12

THE BRAVE MOUSSE, DECK BOY
A nautical story

The voyages on the tall ship "Putnick"
The story of these voyages is told by the tall ship's former
mousse, a young man all of thirteen years old. Years later the
adventurous mousse would become Captain Georges E. Chalonec,
an experienced veteran of the world's seas, licensed by the United
States Coast Guard as Master of United States Steam and Motor
Vessels Unlimted for any Gross Tons upon any Ocean.

Voyages on the tall ship, "Putnick"

PREFACE

A thirteen-year-old boy embarked as a **mousse**, a deck boy, on board the French fishing vessel Putnick, a tall ship. She fished in the North Sea as far as Iceland, via Dunkerque and Norway. One of her most unexpected and potentially lethal catches was an ocean mine!

Without benefit of radar, **Putnick** traversed the stormy, dangerous North Atlantic through fogs and icebergs. In fact, she narrowly avoided the same type of iceberg collision that doomed the **Titanic**. The voyage included the death and burial at sea of a naval officer, with due honors. Through skill and luck, the ship arrived at Newfoundland. Later, she made many journeys from Saint Pierre and Miquelon to the French Antilles, where the Captain sold his fish. The story begins with an introduction of the boy's friends and mentors.

Acknowledgments

I am grateful to Dr. Joyce Dayton, Professor, Indian River Community College, for her exceptional English courses; her good teaching made this book possible.

Special thanks go to Dr. Charles Croghan, Jr., Professor Emeritus, Indian River Community College, for his help and expertise.

To my wife, Marguerite, I would like to express my appreciation for her critique, her help, and her advice.

Captain James J. Brennan, Unlimited Master upon Oceans, and his brother John P. Brennan have given me ample practical help and assistance.

Jean Voza and Roger Dewitt have given me useful help in their critiques and support.

And to my friend Bruno Sainte-Rose, a thirteen-year-old young man, goes my gratitude for his views, critiques, and interest.

THE AUTHOR

Captain Georges E. Chalonec is also the illustrator.

TABLE OF CONTENTS

PART 1
MONSIEUR CARMÉNÉ

onsieur Carméné, besides being a good neighbor, taught me how to use his professional tools and how to be creative; he was a good person and a good friend. In fact, Monsieur Carméné was only a neighbor while I was growing up in Saint Nazaire, France. He was married, and I called his wife Madame Carméné, although I knew her name was Olimp. Madame Carméné called me Paul, short for Paul Agate, one of her husband's uncles whom I resembled. She was in her late twenties, a beautiful, petite woman with lovely, grayish eyes. However, she never wore facial makeup over her smooth, olive skin. She pulled her lustrous brown hair back into a beautiful chignon, and she usually wore large loop gold earrings. Madame Carméné liked chocolates, and she gave me some whenever she had them. She became the talk of the town because she would ride her husband's big, beautiful motorcycle; that was an unusual occurrence in those days. My family was not intimate with them beyond a greeting whenever they crossed each others' paths.

Monsieur Carméné stood about six feet tall—he was a plump man, dark-complexioned with a pleasant face, light green eyes, and two gold front teeth. He was in his thirties when I first met him, and about forty years old when I last saw him. He always kept his working clothes sharp and clean, and he always wore a wide leather belt with a big buckle. Monsieur Carméné was not a smoker. He whistled folk tunes constantly. One of his hobbies was the clarinet, and I enjoyed listening to his playing as much as he enjoyed playing it himself.

Mr. Carméné also called me Paul Agate. He used to arrive home at about 6:00 p.m. every day, and I would be waiting for him at the bottom of the hill because he would put me on the back seat of his motorcycle for the ride home. Occasionally, he would arrive with his truck or his bicycle, and he would put me on the bicycle and push me up the hill.

Monsieur Carméné's friendship and generosity stemmed from his own good nature. He had a carpenter shop in the back of his house; there he taught me how to use tools and how to make my own toys. Of all the toys, I liked the heavy construction dump truck best. It had springs between the wheels and the truck's body, made with metallic banding straps. I could push the truck with a stake and drive it with two strings attached to each side of the front axles. I could also dump any load of material from the truck's body. Making the wheels perfectly round and fitting them to the axles required precision work and measurement, but with Monsieur Carméné's help, I mastered this construction.

Monsieur Carméné provided the materials and showed me how to make a kite. He also taught me how to fly a larger kite called a *ficelle*, which required heavy-duty twine to hold it.

He would put me on the back seat of his
motorcycle for the ride home.

Madame Carméné provided the twine and the colored paper. The kite's body was about thirty-six inches across, and its frame was made with wood slats covered with paper of different colors: red, blue, and yellow. Its tail was about six feet long and made from twine, with pieces of colored rag attached every nine inches. The tail provided a downwind drag that kept the head into the wind. This large, beautiful kite often dragged me on the ground, but I enjoyed every bit of flying it. One day the twine broke, and I watched my beautiful kite disappearing in the white-patched blue sky, and then go down behind the village's church-tower.

Occasionally, I helped Monsieur Carméné with some cabinet making, or with whatever he was building. I was not an apprentice. We enjoyed each other's company; we were just best friends. Thanks to Monsieur Carméné, today I can handle and do anything with carpenter's tools.

Monsieur Carméné was also a good mechanic. Whenever he repaired his truck or his motorcycle, I watched or worked with him. As a result, I picked up some mechanical ability, which helped me later in life. Subsequently, I owned and operated three gasoline stations and repair shops, thanks to Monsieur Carméné, who initiated the first spark of mechanical ability in me.

Of all the toys, I liked the dump truck best.

This larger kite dragged me on the ground.

I last saw Monsieur Carméné when I was fourteen. He and his family died during the bombing of Saint Nazaire during World War ll. I will never forget Monsieur Carméné for his friendship, his patience, and his guidance. Like him, I have helped the young people whom I have met throughout my life. Thus, Monsieur Carméné has left with me his character and his generosity as a model for me to follow.

TIGRESSE

One of my neighbors had two sons, Georges and Léonce, and a beautiful little white and brown dog with a black and white face. His tail was cut off short. Georges and Léonce named the little dog *A Nous Deux* (Between Us Two). I envied them, and I wanted a similar little dog to play with.

Usually I waited for Monsieur Carméné at the bottom of the hill because he would give me a ride home on his motorcycle, but this time, Monsieur Carméné arrived by truck with Captain Colon, a fishing trawler's captain and a friend of Monsieur Carméné and my parents. They picked me up, and I sat between the two of them for the ride home. Captain Colon said, "Joe-Joe, do I have a present for you!" He pulled from his coat pocket a beautiful little dog, similar to *A Nous Deux*, but this one had a long tail. I hugged and kissed the puppy's head, and immediately named him Tiger. When I arrived home, my mother pointed out that Tiger was a female, so I changed her name to Tigresse.

Once I had visited a friend's farm and had seen how the farmer castrated a pig. He tied the pig's legs and muzzle, washed the testicles with soap, and cut them off while another person held the pig down. When it was done, he washed the spot with salt water. I had seen the farmer nail horseshoes directly to the horse's hoof, but to me it appeared to be directly to the horse's foot. It seemed farmers were always doing something to or removing something from every animal they possessed. Since Tigresse had come from a farm, I thought the farmer had forgotten to cut off her tail.

By the end of the summer, Tigresse and I had become the best of friends. But I wanted a dog with a short tail. Early one morning, I washed Tigresse's tail with soap and had my salt water ready, just like the farmer's. I made Tigresse sit and I placed her long tail over a piece of wood. Using a hatchet—pow!—with a single chop, I cut off her long tail. Jet-propelled, Tigresse took off squealing and disappeared. She left me standing surprised with my mouth open, hatchet in hand, the unused salt water still in the bucket. I was in shock at the realization of what I had done to my loving Tigresse. Without a word, I burst into broken cries.

When my mother heard Tigresse's squealing and my crying, she came out. "What happened, Joe-Joe?" she asked. She saw the hatchet in my hand, and Tigress's tail wiggling like a snake over the piece of wood. "What have you done? Ooooh no, you did not do that?" I stood there speechless; I could do nothing but cry. For the rest of the day I searched for Tigresse; she could not be found. By sundown, Tigresse returned home and, whining pitiably, she merely licked the cruel hand that had made her suffer so much. I picked her up, cuddled her, petted her, and thanked her for forgiving me so quickly.

The following morning, my mother took Tigresse to Doctor Julien. After an examination, the doctor said, "Tigresse requires no further treatment."

"Doctor, how much do I owe you?"

"The only payment I want, Madame, is to talk with the boy."

The doctor sat me down and made me promise not to do to any animal what I would not want anyone to do to me, because animals have feelings the same as humans.

Tigresse had short white and brown hair. Half her head was white, the other black, and her four paws were boot-like and brown. She was a small-sized female mutt, with a homemade cutoff short tail. She was not much of a dog for looks, nor was she worth much, but to me she was priceless, beautiful, lovable, faithful, active and intelligent.

She was a good companion. Tigresse was everything I wanted in a dog. Besides their appearances, there was no comparison between her and *A Nous Deux*. *A Nous Deux* hardly participated in anything with Georges or Leonce—maybe they never encouraged him. My parents did not allow Tigresse inside the house, so she grew up an outdoor dog. She was free to roam around and guard the house. She was a good watchdog, but she generally stayed in the backyard or under the porch. My mother took good care of her, and she was a happy dog.

No, No, Tigresse, let go of the ball.

Tigresse followed me wherever I went, except to school or to church — that my mother forbade. However, Tigresse loved to go fishing and swimming, and to play ball with the kids in the water. She never missed a soccer game. Tigresse watched the game and waited for me patiently. One day she jumped into the game and ran with the ball, pushing it along with her muzzle and front feet. Coincidentally, her action favored my team. . Everyone knew her and yelled at her, "No, no, Tigresse, let go of the ball, let go of the ball, Tigresse." The more the kids shouted at her, the faster she ran with the ball. No one could take the ball away from her, but she finally agreed to give me the ball. My team legally won that game. The opposing team refused to admit defeat because they said Tigresse had caused them to lose. One word from our coach, Mr. Bernard, convinced everyone to concede quickly. Not only was Mr. Bernard the head of the stevedores and a rugged individual, but he was also the coach and had donated the complete sports arena.

Eventually, Tigresse got tired of running behind my bicycle. Friends of my parents were fishing people, and we obtained salted fish from them. My mother would send me to another friend who owned a farm, who would exchange vegetables, eggs, butter, or fruit for the salted fish. During World War II, the exchange market was better than the money market. Because I was going to the farm and carrying the fish and farm produce on my bicycle, I attached a large box to the rack on the rear of the bicycle. Naturally, Tigresse would never let me go alone; when I was going downhill, she was running behind the bicycle; when I was going uphill, Tigresse was running in front of the bicycle, and she would wait for me at the top of the hill. I never waited for her at the bottom of the hill. Tigresse had to race with the bicycle on the way down, but she would catch up and pass me before the end of the next upgrade. Finally, Tigresse got tired of running against the bicycle, and to my surprise, she tried to get into the box attached on the back. From then on, I would help her into the box, and she would ride on the bicycle with me. Because the box was full coming from the farm, I had to rig an additional box in the front for Tigresse to sit in.

Tigresse enjoyed the pleasure of the ride, sitting in her box with her head into the wind; but one day she was subjected to the pain of a crash. We were coming from the farm with a load of potatoes on the rear, Tigresse on the front and me on the middle of the bicycle. We were going downhill too fast without any brakes, the brake cable having just broken. I used my feet over the front rubber wheel for a brake, but the soles of my shoes had holes, and they were too thin. My feet were getting hot, and although I alternated them, I could not slow the bicycle any more because of the weight. We usually ran down that hill under similar conditions, but this time it was different.

I had to rig an additional box in front of the bicycle.

In the next few seconds, while going around a bend, we missed a head-on collision with a bus that hugged the road. As a result, we left the road and dived into a semi-dry creek. I remember hearing Tigresse squealing when we crash-landed in the creek, and the next thing I knew she was licking my face and whining while I lay in the water.

Then the bus driver came and picked me up. A woman passenger removed a stone from my knee and bandaged it with the hemline she tore from her white slip. Meanwhile, the bus driver and another passenger straightened the warped bicycle wheels, secured my boxes, and rescued my potatoes. Tigresse and I were back on the bicycle in no time, continuing our trip downhill without any brakes. We arrived home with bruised potatoes, a gouged knee, scraped elbows, and warped wheels.

The following day, my mother discovered a long piece of stick embedded in Tigresse's shoulder. She took Tigresse and me to the only veterinarian available, Dr. Julien. The doctor removed the stick from Tigresse and treated our wounds. After that, Tigresse and I crashed often, which did not stop us from riding the bicycle, with or without a load of potatoes, and sometimes without any brakes. By then, Tigresse's seat had become a permanent fixture in front of my bicycle.

One early spring morning, Tigresse and I went in a nearby *"bois"* (forest) in search of wild mushrooms. While Tigresse was chasing a rabbit, she crossed a small passageway through the woods and was hit by a motorcycle with a side car. Tigresse was badly hurt. I picked her up, and she was bleeding all over me; I was desperately crying and telling her not to die: "*Mon Dieu*, my God, please, Tigresse, do not die." The driver, a German soldier, put us in the side car and drove us to Doctor Julien. The doctor was on call at a nearby farm. Unfortunately, when the doctor arrived, Tigresse had died of her wound. I was inconsolable. The soldier felt so much compassion for Tigresse and me that he drove me home with my dead companion in my arms. My family and some of Tigresse's friends wept over her dead body. Some of my friends and neighbors who heard of Tigresse's death came over to console me. Before sundown, Tigresse was buried in our private backyard. Subsequently, I removed Tigresse's seat from my bicycle, and from then on, I rode alone. The memory of her loving devotion and friendship shall remain with me for the rest of my life.

"Mon Dieu, My God, please Tigresse, don't die."

MONSIEUR BERNARD

Monsieur Bernard was from an important family, and he owned many properties in the community. He was also the head of the Stevedore Association. Everyone knew Monsieur Bernard as a rugged individual because of his fighting on the waterfront. Even children dared not trespass on any of his vacant land.

Monsieur Bernard had two boys: one my age, Paul; the other, Émile, about two years older. He also had a daughter, Flavie, who was older than I. Since I went to school with Paul and Émile, I occasionally played marbles with them in their back yard. I did not care for their unfriendly father. I only wanted to win Paul and Émile's beautiful marbles.

Our marble game started like skittles (bowling) and continued like billiards without the pockets or cues. It was a serious game because we were betting our marbles. The amount we bet was laid in the game, and the winner kept his winnings. Marbles had value depending on their size and quality. The unit of value was one small clay marble, and the number of units in exchange for a better quality marble was agreed upon before the game. For example, one crystal marble was worth five to ten small clay marbles. Usually one out of three games would end in a dispute because children are good winners, but bad losers.

The game in Monsieur Bernard's back yard was going smoothly until I started winning most of the beautiful crystal marbles. Émile and Paul became reluctant to play and tried to repossess their marbles by quickly picking them up. I refused to be intimidated just because they were Monsieur Bernard's sons.

The fight began, but when they saw how determined I was and how furiously I defended myself, they turned tail. Then Flavie came out. The boys must have felt ashamed to chicken out, so they regrouped and attacked me again, but this time Flavie got into the fight to help her brothers. Now it was three against one, and I was no match against them. They managed to get me down. Émile sat on my head holding me down, while Paul and Flavie went through my pockets, taking all my marbles. They did not know yet about my back-up artillery, but they would find out quickly. I then bit Émile's butt, which was on my head. That bite must have hurt him because he yelled and jumped up. I thought they would take my two big steel marbles, so I quickly put them into my mouth. By then, Émile and Flavie had me hanging upside down. Paul was busy picking up the marbles that fell from my pockets. When he came close to me, I grabbed his head and bit his ear. Paul screamed like a pig. That scared his brother and sister, and they dropped me on my head, causing me to swallow the two big steel marbles.

Monsieur and Madame Bernard arrived home simultaneously, and Monsieur Bernard yelled, "What is going on?" Blood was running down from Émile's butt and from Paul's ear, and my clothes were blood-stained with their blood. Monsieur Bernard said to me, "Come here, little boy. What is your name?"

"Georges."

"Who is your parent?"

"Monsieur Chalonec."

"You mean No?"

"Yes sir." (No was my father's nickname.)

"What hurt you?"

"Nothing, sir."

"You have been fighting against three of my children, and nothing hurt you?"

"Nothing hurt me, but your children caused me to swallow two big steel marbles."

"What?"

"I put the marbles in my mouth because they were trying to take them."

"So you're a fighter, and you bite like a dog?"

"No, sir, I bite only when others are beating me."

"I am going to teach you how to fight without biting."

"Yes, sir."

Monsieur Bernard took Émile, Paul, and me to Dr. Julien. The doctor stitched Paul's ear, treated Émile's butt, and told me to use a chamber pot and a stick to search for the marbles

I then bit Emil's butt, which was on my head.

in my stool. Monsieur Bernard brought me home and explained to my mother what had happened. After a week, I found the first marble; it came out shining. I washed it and put it right back in the next game. Ten days later, the second steel marble came out shining, and it, too, went right back into the game.

Monsieur Bernard liked me because I was not a crybaby. Fighting with my five older brothers had toughened me up. The son of Captain Colon, Jean, had enough nerve to play or fight with us, whichever came first. Monsieur Bernard accepted Jean because he was tough, and he knew his father; now he had four boys to teach boxing.

Monsieur Bernard brought home used lumber. All four of us had to clean and remove the old nails from the lumber. New nails could not be found during World War II, so old nails had to be straightened to be used again, which caused many pains when the hammer hit the wrong nail.

With Monsieur Bernard's help, we built a good boxing ring. Then he brought two used pairs of boxing gloves and two sets of headgear. We used an automobile wheel's rim for a bell.

For the next six weeks, twice a week, we did nothing but train to box. Because Émile and Jean were older and taller than Paul and me, they had an advantage, and they beat us every time. Our trainer told us to be patient, and with a little more practice, we should get them. We practiced, but Émile and Jean practiced too, and they still won. Since Monsieur Bernard himself was medium-sized, he decided to get into the ring himself to teach us how to out-maneuver them.

We learned many evasive movements from him, yet we were still not able to beat Émile or Jean. At least, though, we gave them a good run for their money.

One Sunday around noon, after we had dined with Monsieur Bernard, he took us to his attic, where he had a shiny, gray coffin. He told us that he had made it himself for when he dies. Monsieur Bernard opened the coffin and lay down in it for his siesta. We left him in his coffin and went below into the back yard for a good marble game. Now, whenever an altercation occurred during the game, the adversary would get a quick left and a right hook and a bloodied nose, and if that did not work, he would get my reliable back-up artillery.

Just as we were getting good at boxing, a winter storm caused the big shade tree to tumble onto our boxing ring. Clearing the debris from the tree and repairing the ring would require lots of work and time.

Monsieur Bernard had a large, flat, vacant piece of land, which would make a beautiful soccer field. We convinced him to let us use the land to play soccer while we were clearing and repairing the boxing ring. We did not know soccer was his favorite sport; he quickly agreed, and we converted the grassy land into a soccer field. But then Monsieur Bernard wanted part of the team. That caused great difficulties. The children's parents

The Boxing Ring

wanted nothing to do with Monsieur Bernard, and the children were afraid of his lion-sized head and his cleft lip. In addition, not just any kid could join Monsieur Bernard's team. First, he had to be tough, and not a crybaby.

This controversy between Monsieur Bernard, the boys, and their parents made it impossible to organize a soccer team. We could not use the soccer field, and so grass repossessed it. Monsieur Bernard agreed to use my seven goats as automatic lawn mowers to keep the grass down. Meanwhile, we completed clearing all the debris from the fallen shade tree, and we moved the boxing ring into the soccer field.

We resumed boxing, and after a while, Paul defeated Jean and Monsieur Bernard declared a draw between Émile and me. Now the fighting was getting really hot, because the coach often pitted us against each other. Our fighting had improved, and anyone had an even chance to win a fight; the coach was proud of us. But we could not yet recruit enough boys for our soccer team. We requested that the winner from any fight be granted the privilege to sponsor a boy of his own choosing for our soccer team without discrimination. Monsieur Bernard raised his red bushy eyebrows, opened his green cat's eyes, petted his red goatee for a moment, and then agreed. Finally, we managed to organize a junior soccer team, training under Monsieur Bernard's strict discipline.

Now my goats were moved off the field so we could

play. My big, stinking and mean old billy goat never missed an opportunity to butt anyone who got near him. The team named him *"Bélier"* (Ram) and chose him as their mascot. When the kids wanted to have fun with Bélier, they turned him loose in the soccer field; he would run after them, overtake them, and butt them. This billy goat enjoyed the kids as much as the kids enjoyed his chases and his butts. The kids nicknamed Bélier "B. B."—for <u>Bé</u>lier and <u>B</u>ernard, because both had goatees and both were mean, yet both enjoyed kids.

We trained and played soccer against each other for about six months and practiced boxing about every other week. Monsieur Bernard delegated some of his duties in the stevedore company to his lieutenant, so he was free to spend more time with his boys. Consequently, Monsieur Bernard became the talk of the town. Everyone was amazed because he was doing such a good job with the boys. Also, the kids now enjoyed being with him, and they became good friends. Monsieur Bernard kept them off the street; unintentionally, he provided a playground, all the equipment, the soccer field, the boxing ring, and his guidance, all free of charge.

Wind of Monsieur Bernard's benefaction to the boys of our town traveled to other towns. They also heard of his severity and his training. Consequently, we were surprised to receive an invitation and a challenge to play soccer against a proven and more experienced team, the *"Taureau"* (Bull) of Vannes. We accepted the challenge, and the whole town waited impatiently for the proving day. It was not only a test day for the team, but also for Monsieur Bernard and his coaching.

This match was to take place in the opponent's town and on its soccer field. All the parents, relatives, and friends of our team traveled to Vannes to watch the game. We flipped a coin to decide which team would start. The opponent's team won the flip, and they started the game. It was a stiff competition during the first forty-five minutes, and we scored four points each. After the fifteen-minute rest period, the game resumed for another forty-five minutes, but the Bull was beating us: six points for them and four for us. With only thirty minutes to go, we became desperate.

We had to do something to save ourselves. I had noticed their forward center was one of their best players, so I came up with a plan to put him out of the game. Their middle player ran with the ball and kicked it over to my marked boy; I ran after him, and while I was trying to kick the ball away from him, I kicked him a big one right on his ankle. He flipped, tumbled, and rolled over; that quickly put him out of the game. Of course, he was replaced. Now I was hoping his replacement would not be as good as he was.

Within the next fifteen minutes, we were again head-to-head with six points each. We were happy with that, but it looked like we might end with a draw. Just before the game ended, we scored a last point against them: six points for Bull and seven points for our Ram. We rejoiced in having won our first game and, at the same time, our first victory. Our Ram was meaner than their Bull—and so was our billy goat, B. B., who never missed an opportunity to butt or kick someone's ankle! The other B. B., Bernard, our coach, was so proud. He became speechless and appeared about to weep, but he did not, and he laughed and laughed joyfully.

That evening we returned home. The town cheered for the team, as well for Monsieur Bernard and his coaching, both being under the town's scrutiny. Monsieur Bernard had vindicated himself, and now he was recognized as one of the town's most prominent citizens.

Three weeks after our glorious conquest, we received another challenge from the *"Loup"* (Wolf) of Nantes Junior High School. This long-established team had beaten the Bull of Vannes, our last conquest. We accepted the challenge, and the match was scheduled in two weeks, but this time in our town and on our soccer field. Our town was full of curiosity and doubts. Some adults, especially those associated with Mr. Bernard's stevedore company, started taking bets for or against the Wolf. The betting caused concern and, again, we became the talk of the town.

The day of the game finally came, and our opponent, the soccer team Wolf, arrived at our field. The area around the field was filled to capacity, and people who had brought their own

BéLier, B.B. The Mascot, which never missed an opportunity to butt anyone who got near him!

seats were unable to locate a spot. Finally, the game started and went on brutally.

This team was ferocious. About halfway through the game, they broke the arm of our goalie, and we were head to head, three points each. Since the opponents were so tough and brutal, Monsieur Bernard warned us to be extra careful and to protect ourselves as he had taught us. With only twenty minutes left until the end of the game, Jean, one of our players, was attempting to score a point. Their front defense blocked the ball and stopped Jean from scoring the point. But Jean kicked his knee and down he went—yet their fans clapped and applauded his action as he was carried out. Because Jean's point was blocked, the game ended in a draw: three points each. The Wolf broke our goalie's arm, but his ferocity was not enough to intimidate our B. B.!

Our team felt that most of the credit and praise was due to our coach. We picked him up, carried him on our shoulders, and shouted, "Thank you, Monsieur Bernard, thanks a million!" Then the spectators clapped and clapped their hands, and yelled *"Vive, Monsieur Bernard."* (Long live Monsieur Bernard.)

The town council and the school board recognized Monsieur Bernard's accomplishment and leadership. The two soccer teams we played against were from two nearby towns, and coached by their schools. Our town, which was about the same size, did not have a sports program. Monsieur Bernard's accomplishment pointed out these facts, and the need for such a program. He alone had created, operated, and financed a sports program for our town's kids.

After a few weeks, the town's Mayor and the School Board conferred with Monsieur Bernard, and their exchange of views brought mutual understanding. Arrangements were made between the town and Monsieur Bernard to transfer the sport's stadium deed to the town and its management to the school board. The Mayor seated Monsieur Bernard as an honorary member on the town council, and the School Board kept him as head coach of their new sports program. The town added tennis courts and named the sports arena "Bernard's Sport Stadium."

Bernard's Sport Stadium

"Vive, Monsieur Bernard, Long Live Monsieur Bernard."

PART II
VOYAGE 1
MADAME LÉOPOLD

Everyone in town addressed her as Madame Léopold. She stood six feet tall, a beautiful two-hundred pound Creole woman. She was a medium, a spirit guide, from French Guiana. Monsieur Léopold, her husband, a dark complexioned man slightly over five feet tall and weighing about one hundred fifty pounds, owned a 185-foot fishing vessel...a tall ship. He was the Captain, and Captain Colon was the Staff Captain.

When my parents lived in Saint Nazaire, France, Monsieur and Madame Léopold were good neighbors. They had four children: Lazar, five years older than I; the twins, Hilde and Hildelite, who were younger than I; and Socrate, a baby boy. The family lived in an expensive two-story house, having become wealthy in land speculation and gold mining in Guiana.

Madame Léopold went to church and received Holy Communion every morning; she also taught the catechism. As a well-known medium, she gave remedies for an optional fee and charged nothing for those who could not afford the fee. Her clairvoyant practices caused controversy among the parishioners. Most of the people gossiped about a sorceress who taught the catechism and used the church for her personal reasons. But they were all afraid to confront Père Cèsaire, the parish priest, because no one wanted to do the teaching. During my time, only Madame Léopold volunteered and taught the catechism to me and the rest of the children.

Madame Léopold operated a séance from eight to five daily, except Sundays, holidays, and Thursdays when she taught the catechism. People filled her waiting room to see her. Also, some sick people would come to see her as a last resort after receiving a negative prognosis from medical doctors. When the sick person could not come, a parent or a friend would come with an object, usually a piece of clothing the sick person had worn. If for any reason the person was unable to write, Madame Léopold would call me to write the prescription. She did not write during a séance, although sometimes she breast-fed her baby.

Madame Léopold would sit and calmly close her eyes while holding the object that belonged to the sick person. Then she would fall into a trance and reveal the illness or the reason for the visit. Next, she dictated simple herbal remedies or medicines that could be obtained from any pharmacy without a doctor's prescription. Occasionally, sick people were referred to a doctor after they had been told the cause of their illness.

I wrote prescriptions for hundreds of séances, and I never witnessed any oddities that might be related to the occult. Madame Léopold was a good person who used her God-given ability to cure illnesses only for those who sought her help. She was a good clairvoyant, and not a sorceress. Sometimes after the person had left, I would ask Madame Léopold to look into my future. She predicted that I would make many long voyages over seas, that I would live most of my life in a greater nation than France, and that I would have a very long and successful life.

By the side of a large pond covered with water lilies stood our church, an old wooden building, badly maintained because of the small and scanty offerings from the parishioners. Madame Léopold donated most of her séance monies to the parish priest, a licensed architect, to build quickly the only movie theater in the area. The new movie theater provided lots of revenue, and an additional donation from Monsieur and Madame Léopold made it possible to build a beautiful new, white, concrete church with a high clock and bell tower that dominated the area. An anonymous benefactor donated the clock and all the bells for the church's tower. Business people donated the doors and flooring: tile, carpet, and marble. In an all-out effort to complete the new church, the parish children collected enough money for the necessary furniture, benches, and stained glass windows. All the fishing boat owners and their crews offered the harmonium and statues of their patron saints, and the new church was completed just before World War II.

Père Césaire, the parish priest, scheduled the dedication of the new church to coincide with the children's celebration of their First Communion, the best celebrated days in a child's life.

The New Church

In the old days, First Communion required a special costume for both child and escort. For this occasion, Madame Léopold made me a traditional navy blue suit, my very first new clothing. Since the day I was born, I had worn hand-me-downs from my five older brothers. On that Sunday, the Bishop came to dedicate the new church and celebrated the Communion ceremony, so I received the Sacrament from the Bishop. Bishops do not usually participate in a child's First Communion. Madame Léopold was dressed in a very chic Creole costume, decorated with beautiful Creole gold jewels. She escorted me to my First Communion with my new clothing and new shoes. I felt distinguished, like a prince in a fairy tale.

After the church's ceremony, my escort and I returned home for coffee, chocolate milk, and a special butter loaf. Then she took me for the traditional calls to relatives and friends, after which we returned home for the festive dinner. My parents butchered one of my goats, and Captain Léopold supplied and prepared the excellent seafood. After a delicious meal and fine wines, the family and guests toasted me with champagne to wish me the best in life.

Captain Léopold jokingly said to my mother, "Désirée, we should marry your Joe-Joe to my daughter, Hildelite. You would bring straight hair, and I would bring money." (Beautiful Hildelite had curly hair.)

"Oh! Captain, indeed, that would be nice!"

Everyone smiled with approval, and Madame Léopold sang "Ave Maria," accompanied by her husband on his violin. Everybody applauded, and the festivity ended.

She escorted me, and I felt distinguished

When school closed for summer vacation, Captain Léopold took me for a six-week voyage on board his beautiful tall ship, *Putnick*, a sail and engine fishing vessel. On the way to the fishing ground, we trolled (trailing fishing lines with hooks, baits, or lures). At alternate fishing grounds, we dragged for scallops, crabs, or shrimp; we also did some gill-netting and seining. I enjoyed all the various types of fishing, but was most overjoyed steering the tall sailing vessel; she had to be steered by compass, and her sails had to be kept filled with wind.

After three weeks of fishing, *Putnick*'s freezer and fish holds were filled. The crew was happy because they received shares from the catch's value, not fixed salaries; they told the captain that I brought them good luck. On the way back home, we trolled again until we encountered inclement weather. Captain Léopold ordered all sails down, except one small storm sail that reduced the ship's rolling, and we continued on our way home with the engine only. The swells became so high that they appeared like mountains, rolling toward us and crashing over the deck. The ship rose above one mountain and dove into a deep trough, as deep as the previous mountains. With each rapid up and down, I felt my buttocks rising to my mouth and squeezing every drop of food out of my stomach. My eyes teared, my nose plugged, and my head ached; my throat got irritated, so I wanted to drink, but the more I drank, the more I threw up. This was my first and my last seasickness; I will never forget the terrible feeling.

After the weather improved, Captain Léopold ordered most of the sails up, but trimmed; their sizes were reduced by attached trim lines. We made good headway with the sails trimmed. When the sea and swell calmed, Staff Captain Colon

**Madame Léopold sang "Ave Maria," accompanied
by her husband on his violin.**

ordered all hands on deck and ready to come about. This order
meant for everyone to prepare the ship for tacking; that is,
heading the ship's bow into the wind and putting the sails on the
opposite side. Following this maneuver, he ordered all sails up
and engine full speed ahead in an effort to arrive home before
sunset. We made good speed on the port tack (wind on port or

left side, and sails on starboard or right side), until the change of watch after 8:00 A.M. When *Putnick* dove into a freakish trough with a sudden gusty wind, the top sail mast parted and tumbled onto the deck. Captain Colon ordered all hands on deck to recover the loose sail, clear the deck, secure the broken piece of the mast, and make the ship seaworthy again. We continued on our way home, but arrived after sunset, too late for docking. We spent the rest of the night anchored in home port waters.

Early in the morning, we docked at the fishing pier, and the dock workers came aboard to unload our cargo. Shortly after the discharge commenced, Monsieur Chenard, the stevedores' boss, got into an argument with Monsieur Charlot, the ship's boatswain, because the stevedores were mishandling the cargo, some of which fell overboard into the water. First, they yelled at each other; then Chenard punched the boatswain, causing his mouth to bleed. Then the real fight began. Captain Léopold heard the commotion; he interrupted the fight and chased Chenard off the ship. Chenard became enraged and punched the Captain in the face, broke his eyeglasses, and made his face bleed. Staff Captain Colon called the *"gendarmes"* (police), and all the stevedores walked off the ship. All these disturbances terrified me, so I jumped on a bicycle parked on the dock and rushed to Madame Léopold's house. On my arrival, she picked me up, hugged me, kissed me, and said, "Now, Joe-Joe, tell me what happened?"

"Mr. Chenard has beaten Captain Léopold!"

"What?"

"He punched the Captain's face, and broke his eyeglasses."

"Is that all?"

"The Captain's face is bleeding."

"Oh, no! No!"

She jumped in her car, and said, "Get in Joe-Joe; forget the bicycle." We raced to the pier. Unfortunately for Chenard, Madame Léopold saw him first. She grabbed him, raised him up, and slammed him on the concrete pier. Then she jumped all over him, stomping him down. During Chenard's beating, Monsieur Bernard, the President of the Stevedore Company, conferred on board with Captain Léopold and apologized to him. Monsieur Bernard and the Captain heard the commotion on the dock, so they ran to investigate. However, it was too late for Chenard; he could not move from the concrete floor. Monsieur Bernard ordered one of his men to call an ambulance. When Madame Léopold saw her husband on the dock with his bandaged face, she cried out, "Léopold, Léopold, *mon chéri.*" (my darling.) Then she hugged and kissed him.

The ship rose above one high swell and
dove into a deep trough.

The stevedores resumed cargo operations under the supervision of the Staff Captain. Captain Léopold, his wife, and I got in the car, and they brought me home. First, my mother tried to hug me alone, but my brothers and sisters interfered, so all of them hugged and kissed me together.

After my mother greeted us, she said to the Captain, "Did Joe-Joe cause you any trouble during the voyage?"

"No, The only trouble he caused was to himself."

"What was that, Captain?"

"Joe-Joe got seasick. But it soon passed, and I enjoyed sailing with him."

They stayed only for a brief visit and went home. Next, my mother said, "Now let me take a good look at you; did you have a good time on board the ship? The food must have been good, because you gained a little weight. You have a good suntan, and you look like a real seaman."

My brothers and sisters had different questions. "Did you catch many fish or sharks? How big? Did you see any whales, porpoises, or dolphins?" They wanted me to describe the big storm that broke the ship's mast, how I felt being seasick, and Chenard's beating. They asked for it, and they got it—a tall tall tale!

The following morning, I rode the bicycle back to the pier and found out the bike belonged to Monsieur Chenard. In the afternoon, his son came and picked up the bicycle; he did not even know that I had used it to turn Madame Léopold loose on his father. Captain Colon told us that Chenard had several bruises and two broken ribs.

After completing the cargo discharging, we shifted the ship to a shipyard for repairs. Finally, school reopened, and my vacation ended. Captain Léopold said, "Joe-Joe, you were a good shipmate, and you will be welcome on board on your next vacation."

At Chenard's beating, she jumped and stomped all over him.

My brothers and sisters, they asked for it and they
got it all—a tall, tall tale!

VOYAGE II
DUNKERQUE, FRANCE

After school reopened, the way of life changed rapidly. Schools became congested and were constantly interrupted by World War II. As a result, I was not in school half of the time. · I used this free time playing nearby or exploring in dangerous areas, far away from home, on my bicycle.

It was necessary to change the method of my education for my welfare. The big question was what to do with me. I decided that I wanted to become a Marine Officer. In those days, the best nautical school was on board a ship. The parents would choose a good ship's Captain; then for a monthly fee (or sometimes without any fee), the captain would take the boy on board his ship as an apprentice and educate him. For a government diploma, the time served on board ship counted as required sea time. In my case, the decision was easy for my family because Madame Léopold participated in the decision-making. Her husband, Captain Léopold, and his assistant Captain Colon were happy to have me as their new apprentice.

My mother and Captain Léopold went to City Hall where he then became my legal guardian. The following day, I embarked as a *"mousse,"* (a deck boy), on board the *Putnick*. I felt at home among all my friends: Monsieur Charlot, the boatswain; Monsieur De Montaigne, the chief engineer; and recently embarked, my old friend Monsieur Carméné, the ship's carpenter. Consequently, I became part of *Putnick*'s crew; I was now a real seaman. I felt great pride in doing the duties assigned to me, and the entire crew encouraged me.

For accommodations, I shared a small cabin with Foo, the cook. I ate with the petty officers, the boatswain and the carpenter. I also served their meals, and I was in charge of the petty officers' mess hall. In the morning, I worked in the galley with Foo, and in the afternoon with the boatswain or the carpenter, and sometimes with the engineer in the engine room. The boatswain did not work in the morning because he stood the dog's watch, midnight to four in the morning. I enjoyed all the different duties and became the crew's pet. Every one of them instructed and helped me and took me on several short fishing trips nearby. Then we went to the shipyard for compulsory annual inspection and the required repairs to the ship and its fishing gear. During the shipyard stay, Captain Colon gave me a week off and two books, grammar and mathematics, to study while at home.

Customarily, after an annual refitting, a fishing vessel usually goes on a long fishing voyage because it is more seaworthy and has better gear. This longer fishing voyage might help compensate for the costly annual refitting. So, after the refitting, we stored and stocked the ship for sea and prepared for a long fishing voyage to the North Sea. Waiting for final parts and sea stores, we shifted the ship to the anchorage near the shipyard. While at anchorage, the crew painted the ship dark gray, the wartime color, which made it less visible.

During my week off at home, I had lots of fun with my brothers and sisters. My mother also spoiled me a little more than usual, but she made sure that I did the homework Captain Colon had given me. On Monday morning, Madame Léopold drove my mother, Captain Léopold, and me to the shipyard. We hugged and kissed goodbye, and Captain Léopold and I boarded the motor boat that took us to the ship. I could see my mother and Madame Léopold waving with their handkerchiefs as the motorboat took us away from them. On board the ship, Captain Colon started heaving up the anchor chain. When we got on board, the anchor was already aweigh, and we sailed off. With my handkerchief, I continued waving goodbye to my mother and Madame Léopold until they faded away in the distance.

While trolling, we sailed northbound along the coast of France, and while doing various types of fishing, we hove to (the ship was headed into the wind or current, but remained stationary). We dragged and fished along the French side of the English Channel until we were about to enter the North Sea.

When the boatswain heaved up a fishing net, an all-out cry broke out: "A mine, a mine in the net, a mine in the net!" Captain Colon came out running and yelling, "Stop, stop whatever you are doing. Hold steady on what you have in your hands. Wait, hold on steady and wait." Then he asked, "Now, where is the mine?"

I could see my mother and Madame Léopold waving with their handkerchiefs; I continued waving goodbye to them until they faded away.

Captain Colon quickly had the bottom of the net up, using another tackle, and the mine hung safely in the nets. After we wrapped it with another net, we lashed the mine so it could not move in any direction. Once we stabilized it securely, Captain Colon organized a mine watch. Then Captain Léopold ordered first, that all fishing gear and all sails be secured, and second, that all hands below knock off, except those on mine and navigation watches.

Lucky for us, the mine did not explode in our fishing net. We continued on our way to Dunkerque using the engine only, and without any fishing. Once more we were lucky, because *Putnick's* freezers were fully loaded with various types of fish, crabs and scallops. We arrived in the port of Dunkerque in the North Sea in the early morning, with our big catch and our mine. The port authority kept us outside at anchor the whole day, until mine experts defused the mine and took it away. The ship docked immediately that evening and unloaded its cargo of fish. Food is a necessity; farming and fishing must continue peacetime or wartime. The following day the crew was happy, for they received their shares from the cash value of the fish sold. Captain Léopold gave them a night and a day off to send their money home or put it in the bank, and they enjoyed life in that beautiful port.

On arrival at the dock, my friend Émile, the son of Monsieur Bernard, joined the crew as a "novice." Captain Colon assigned Émile a bunk bed in the foxhole, the crew's quarter. Émile, who never liked school, did not want to study, so he would share in the fish cash value according to his rating and ability. I did not receive a share, only a small monthly salary. Émile replaced me in the galley in the morning, and worked with the boatswain in the afternoon. Now, I worked and studied with Captain Colon in the morning and with the boatswain in the afternoon.

The following day, we stored and stocked the ship for sea: food, water, diesel fuel and coal. We added two extra bins on deck to carry extra coal. We also added two spare fuel tanks and loaded on deck a dozen diesel fuel drums; they were well-secured with lumber and wire, and covered with a wire net to keep them from floating away when heavy seas flooded the deck. Finally, the engineer completed the installation of two salt water distillers to the ship's main engine and the diesel generator. Also, we installed two water tanks where hot distilled water cooled off. The crew had another night off to enjoy the last port in France. Hoping we did not catch another mine, we were ready and willing for some serious North Sea fishing.

Dunkerque, *Putnick* at Anchor outside waiting
for experts to diffuse the mine.

Dunkerque, *Putnick* docked

VOYAGE III
BERGEN, NORWAY

Not only did the crew enjoy Dunkerque, the last port in France, but also they went shopping for their favorite cheeses, *"saucissons"* (sausages), and wines. Everyone bought additional foul weather gear. Also, local sail makers completed the repairs to our sails.

The following morning, we sailed for the North Sea fishing area and Bergen, Norway. But we were all afraid of catching another sea mine with our fishing nets. As a result, Captain Léopold added a mine watch to the navigation watch. Our first couple of days in the North Sea, we sailed northward with the warm current astern, while towing fishing lines. We spotted a large school of fish, which proved to be bounteous; it gave us a big catch.

Soon we changed our course to northeast. Keeping the current abaft the beam (a line perpendicular to the keel line of the ship), we continued trolling and searching for schools of fish. We also kept a sharp lookout for mines. The trolling proved to be beneficial; we caught many big fish.

Thereafter, the sea became choppy for the next two days, and Émile got seasick. Émile threw up so much that he became weak and unable to work. During his seasickness, I replaced him in the galley with Foo, the cook. I also discovered that Foo was an amateur boxer. He had two pairs of boxing gloves in his sea bag, a new pair and a used, torn pair.

Although we wanted to keep the warm current astern for best speed and good fishing, we had to stay away from adjacent prohibited territorial fishing ground and from ships' traffic lanes. Also, we could fish only during daylight hours, for we maintained complete darkness between sunset and sunrise. In addition, we could not afford to be spotted by either force, the enemy or the ally, because a sail fishing vessel built of wood and properly equipped would make a perfect decoy, or spy ship, for detecting the enemy's forces in the water or in the air.

Consequently, we changed our course to north and headed for the southern end of Norway. The weather became stormy. Captain Colon ordered the safety wires to be stretched on both sides of the deck from the bow to the stern. He also instructed the crew to use their safety belts whenever required to be on deck from then on. (The safety belt hook slides on the safety wire; the seaman then slides from the bow to the stern without being washed overboard by the heavy sea.)

After obtaining our noon position, Captain Colon ordered all hands on deck and ready to go about. The order meant to prepare the ship for tacking, change the ship's head toward the wind, and put the sails on the opposite side. At that time, the deck was awash. During this maneuver, Émile did not wear his safety belt as instructed, so a big swell crashed over the deck and took Émile into the stormy cold sea. The boatswain yelled, "Man overboard, man overboard!"

Captain Colon shouted, "Belay the order to go about. Belay the ready to go about. Steady as she goes. Steady as she goes." Then he yelled, "All hands look for the man. All hands look for the man."

We spotted Émile's head bobbing up and down above a swell.

Then Captain Colon ordered, "Emergency crew, prepare to launch the emergency motor life boat." Captain Colon commanded the emergency crew, so he joined his crew in the boat. Captain Léopold maneuvered the ship, with the engine only, to a position upwind from Émile and created a "lee"—a calm area sheltered from the wind or sea by the ship's body—for the launching of the lifeboat. Then Captain Léopold ordered: "Ready to launch the boat on my order. Wait for my 'Now'."

At the proper synchronization between the ship and the swells, he yelled "Ready-y-y-y... Now." Quickly the crew lowered the boat into the water; then it simply drifted downwind to Émile and the rescuers plucked him out of the cold water. Meanwhile, Captain Léopold maneuvered the ship to a position downwind from Émile and the rescue boat. Then the boat drifted to the ship. The lifeboat crew and Émile climbed on board using a rope cargo net, which had been previously placed over the ship's side to facilitate their boarding. The boat could not be retrieved because of the heavy sea, so we towed it all night.

The next morning, we secured the emergency lifeboat in its stored position between the davits. Then Captain Léopold called all hands on deck and reprimanded Émile for not wearing his safety belt as instructed. He also reminded everyone of the importance of the safety belt and when it was required to be worn.

Captain Léopold created a "lee"—a calm area sheltered from the wind or sea by the ship's body—for the launching of the lifeboat.

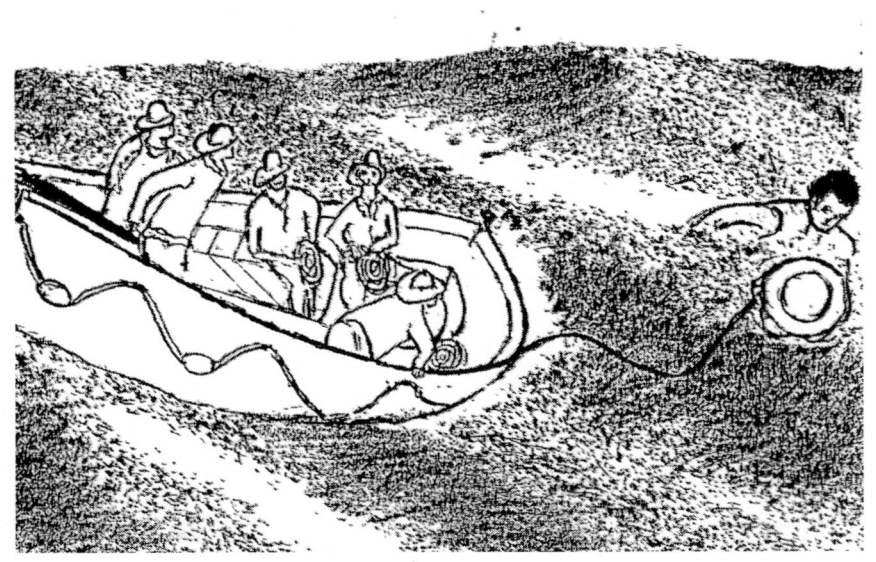

The rescuers plucked Émile out of the cold water.

Towing fishing lines and seining whenever we spotted a school of fish, we continued our way north. The weather cleared and the sea calmed. Because we fished only during daylight and we could not fish anywhere, *Putnick*'s freezers were only three-quarters full. Our catch was not as big as the one on arrival at Dunkerque; but lucky for us, we had not caught another mine.

By now, everyone knew that Foo had boxing gloves, and that three amateur boxers were on board: Foo, Émile, and myself, Georges. The crew wanted a little recreation, so they asked the boatswain to ask Captain Colon's permission to have a boxing match on Sunday afternoon. The captain agreed, provided that no hard head blows were allowed because we did not have headgear. The boatswain promised to be the referee, and anyone who threw a hard head blow would be disqualified. The crew quickly converted the hatch cover into a boxing ring, and Foo's frying pans became the bell. The first fight would be between Émile and me; the winner would have a second fight against Foo, the cook. If he won both fights, a purse of 250 francs would . be his winning. If Foo won the second fight, the purse would be divided between them, 125 francs each. The crew had various bets among themselves. The first of four rounds was scheduled to start in fifteen minutes.

The announcer introduced the first fight: "In one corner stands Georges, the *mousse*, weighing sixty kilos (132 pounds), jumping and punching his corner ring rope; Monsieur Carméné is his coach. In the other corner stands Émile, the novice, weighing sixty-two kilos (136 ponds), pulling, and jumping on the ring rope; Monsieur De Montaigne is his coach."

Then the announcer added, "Near the bell stands Boatswain Charlot, the Referee."

Next the referee declared: "No hard head blows will be allowed; anyone who throws a hard head blow will be disqualified by order of the captain." Then he shouted, "When the bell rings, come out fighting."

The bell rang, and the first of four rounds started. I danced, skipped, and avoided Émile's punches. I threw a few punches at him, but he blocked or evaded most of them. I tangled with him, so I could recover. He was beating me, and, at last, I was saved by the bell. I returned to my corner. Monsieur Carméné covered me with a wool blanket to protect me against the cool air, and he advised me how to hit and to evade Émile's punches.

Émile yelled, "He bit me. He bit me."

The bell rang and the second round started. I landed a few punches on Émile, but he hit me with a medium head blow that caused me to see stars. We tangled, and Émile being taller than I, he quickly had me in a headlock. While blocking the referee's view, he punched my face, hard and rapidly. I became furious, and I bit his armpit. Émile screamed and immediately let go of my head. Then he yelled, "He bit me. He bit me." The referee stopped the fight, disqualified me, and called Émile the winner.

During the half-hour recess, Émile had some refreshments, and his coach prepared him for his second fight against Foo, the cook. To warm up, the spectators drank a few glasses of wine, ate cheese and sausage, and sipped some hot bouillabaisse.

The second fight was about to start, and the announcer introduced the fighters: "In one corner stands Émile, the champion, weighing sixty-two kilos (136 pounds), pulling on the rope and squatting; Monsieur De Montaigne is his coach. In the other corner stands Foo, the contender, weighing sixty-four kilos (139 pounds), dancing and jumping; Monsieur Carméné is his coach."

The referee declared: "No hard head blow is allowed. When the bell rings, come out fighting."

The bell rang and the first of four rounds started. Both fighters fought aggressively, but the first and second rounds were draws. Foo won the third and fourth rounds by only a point or so each, but Émile fought well and intensively. The entire fight should have been called a draw. The judge gave the fight to Foo, but most of the men insisted that Émile had won the fight. Émile called the decision unfair and requested a rematch. The crew had a good time, which was the purpose of these fights, and the fighters fought well.

While fishing, we continued on our way north. During the war most European countries maintained complete darkness at night; therefore, Captain Léopold adjusted departure and arrival so they occurred only during daylight hours. Early Monday morning, we made landfall at the southern end of Norway. Captain Colon ordered all fishing gear secured and the deck cleared to avoid any accusation of fishing in Norwegian territorial water. Just before sunset that evening, we arrived at the port of Bergen, Norway, where pilotage was compulsory. The Norwegian pilot guided *Putnick* to the dock, and our cargo would be discharged in the morning during daylight hours. However, local authority granted the crew shore liberty, and Captain Léopold gave them a draw in Norwegian money. After two weeks at sea, the crew took full advantage of Norwegian hospitality. Indeed, they had a good time in that beautiful and clean city, where the people were so friendly.

The next morning, everyone was on board for a meeting. Because of war-related causes, we might lose the ship to the ally or the enemy. The crew voted two to one not to return home, and to continue on our North Atlantic crossing to *"Terre-Neuve"* (Newfoundland), where two small French islands, Saint Pierre and Miquelon, had fishing rights. The time of the year was right to arrive at Newfoundland, before the hurricane season and the icebergs' peak drifting season.

After taking on board new sea store, food, and fuel— and we did not forget the wine—the crew had two full nights and one day to enjoy the Norwegian life and to do their private shopping. At sunrise the following day, we were scheduled to sail for Newfoundland.

VOYAGE IV
REYKJAVIK, ICELAND

On a Wednesday morning, we sailed from Bergen, Norway, for the North Atlantic crossing westward to Newfoundland, Canada. Because of a strong southwest wind, we steered northwest for our first course. This course would take us clear north from the Shetland and the Faroe Islands. We knew about the British blockade, and knew we might not be able to go west passing south of these islands without British obstruction.

After the ship settled on her first course, I realized that I was on my way to Canada and not on my way home because the crew had voted against returning to France. They did not allow my vote, for I was only thirteen years old. Two months ago, I had left home; I was now homesick. Thoughtfully, I sat over a coiled heap of rope, my chin resting on my hand and my elbow resting on my knee. The boatswain and Monsieur Carméné noticed my sadness. Sympathetically, they approached me and asked me, "*Mousse*, what is the matter?"

That question caused me to explode into a fit of weeping with my mouth wide open: "*Je veux ma maman. Je veux ma maman.*" (I want my Mother. I want my Mother.)

"Mousse, what is the matter?" Then Captain Léopold
shouted, "I want you to be a brave Mousse!"

Captain Léopold came out and yelled at me for the first time. "Stop; stop that sissy, silly crying immediately. What kind of seaman are you?" Then he shouted, "I want you to be *a brave mousse, a brave mousse,* and that is an order." That was the last time I cried out or wept. Then *"The Brave Mousse, Deck boy"* became this book's title.

We continued this northwest course for approximately five hours until we spotted a British patrol boat, a submarine chaser, combing the area. Because we were a wooden sailing vessel, its radar might not have picked us up; in addition, its sonar would not detect us, for we navigated by sail only and had no engine running. Moreover, the patrol boat might not have seen us visually, either, so we quickly changed our course to north and immediately commenced fishing, towing purse nets (a net consisting of one long pocket and a wide mouth which can be quickly closed). This north course indicated a destination other than Canada.

Because her radar or sonar equipment did not detect us, the patrol boat might have suspected we were a spy ship. She observed us until just before sunset; then she contacted us using Morse code, blinker light. The patrol boat requested our name, port of registry, and our itinerary. We answered: *"Putnick,* Saint Nazaire, on a fishing voyage to Iceland via Bergen, Norway, and return to France." The British might have been observing us since we left Dunkerque, and our identity confirmed our activity.

We continued our north course fishing, hugging the Norwegian coast. During the night, the patrol boat observed us, but we could barely discern her silhouette on the horizon. However, in the morning, the patrol boat had disappeared. Either she had more urgent business elsewhere, or her captain believed that our return voyage to France would be a more appropriate time to seize our ship and equip her as a spy ship.

Our new course took us further north than we had expected to go. We changed our course to northwest to pass north of the Faroe Islands with a wide berth (adequate distance), and we continued our fishing. We never saw so many codfish; we could almost catch them with our bare hands. By now, *Putnick's* freezers were full with codfish, and we did not know yet what to do with them.

Then Captain Léopold decided we would make an unexpected call to Reykjavik, Iceland, approximately thirty hours away. At noon, the Faroe Islands bore south of us, and we changed our course to west. We observed another patrol boat, but it ignored us. The sea and swell were calm, and *Putnick's* freezers were full of fish; consequently, Captain Colon ordered all fishing gear secured and the deck cleared. Then he ordered all sails up and the engine full speed ahead in an effort to arrive the next day before sunset. In Reykjavik, we could sell our cod fish for whatever price we could get and pick up some fresh sea store; we could also use some recreation.

After arrival in Reykjavik, the ship remained at anchor that night and the whole next day. Captain Léopold went ashore in the morning, sold our fish for a good price, and returned on board. Immediately, we docked that evening, and the captain gave the crew a draw in Icelandic money, so they took off to town, except those in port watches. In the morning, the longshoremen discharged our cargo and brought on board fresh provisions: vegetables, meat, and wine. We also filled our tanks with diesel fuel and fresh water and our bins with coal. The crew had another night to enjoy the marvelous Icelandic hospitality. Captain Léopold scheduled our departure, for the second time, to Newfoundland, at sunrise the following morning.

Because her radar or sonar did not detect us, the patrol boat might have suspected we were a spy ship.

VOYAGE V

BELLE ISLE
NEWFOUNDLAND, CANADA

From Reykjavik, Iceland, once more we sailed for the North Atlantic crossing to Newfoundland, where Saint Pierre and Miquelon had French fishing rights. Upon clearing the port, we encountered a strong northeast wind (wind and currents are named for the direction from which they come). Since we wanted to go south, we put the wind astern for best speed, and we steered south for warmer weather. Wanting to get away from the cold Icelandic weather, and also to avoid the path of the North Atlantic icebergs, we would hold to this south course for as long as necessary, weather permitting.

During our first night at sea, just before dawn, one of the most spectacular displays among celestial phenomena greeted us: the Aurora Borealis, or Northern Lights. (A similar phenomenon in the Southern Hemisphere is called the Aurora Australis). Auroras are the most visible effect of the sun's activity on the earth's atmosphere. When the sun's electrically charged particles are trapped by the earth's magnetic field, they travel toward the earth's magnetic poles and appear as auroras—mostly as arcs, clouds, and streaks. The most common color is green, but displays sometimes may be red or purple.

The Aurora Borealis or Northern Lights. The most common color is green, but it may be red or purple.

Wind and Swells Astern:
"Putnick" **surfed South for warmer weather.**

The aurora that greeted us arose as a spectacular overture, a welcoming celebration for our approach to the New World. This phenomenon became visible just before dawn, a continuous array of luminous arcs splendidly arranged in shades of green with a splash of red. Where the green and the red merged, the lights appeared yellowish with flickering bright white streaks. The Aurora covered almost half of the celestial dome, and stayed with us until just before sunrise. However, it disturbed our magnetic compass and caused its needle to spin away from the north magnetic pole, but we continued steering south by using the North Star or other constellations as reference points. The following night, we did not see the aurora because of a solid overcast sky, and our magnetic compass gradually stabilized.

With the wind and swells astern, the ship seemed to surf and speed toward the south for the next two days. Then the wind backed around to the southwest from the stern to the port bow. (It is said to "back around" when the wind changes direction in a counter-clockwise manner). Captain Colon ordered all hands on deck and ready to come about. (The order meant all hands prepare the ship for tacking; that is, direct the ship's head toward the wind and put the sails on the opposite side). We were happy with this southwest wind; first, it warmed us quickly; second, it slowed our speed, which allowed us to do some fishing and eat fresh fish. We approached the position where we would begin to head west-southwest, across the icebergs' path and on to Newfoundland.

The crew took advantage of the warmer weather and asked Captain Colon permission to give Émile, the novice, his boxing rematch against Foo, the cook, a small Indo-Chinese man. The captain agreed to let them have some fun, providing no hard head blows were allowed. That afternoon, again they converted the hatch cover into a boxing ring and used Foo's frying pan as a bell. A purse of 300 francs would be the winner's reward. Furthermore, the crew had bet among themselves. In five minutes, the first of the six rounds would start.

The announcer introduced the fighters and their coaches in their respective corners; then he introduced Monsieur Charlo, the boatswain, as the referee. Next the referee shouted: "No hard head blows will be allowed; anyone who throws a hard head blow will be disqualified by order of the captain." Then he added, "When the bell rings, come out fighting."

The bell rang and the first of the six rounds began. Foo won the first and third rounds, and Émile triumphed in the second and fourth. Because both fighters appeared exhausted, the referee decided to increase the rest period between rounds. The bell rang, and the fifth round started; both fighters fought well. Suddenly, Émile knocked out Foo with a forbidden hard head blow! The referee stopped the fight, disqualified Émile, and named Foo the winner. Foo welcomed the 300-franc prize. After a rest period, he returned to the galley and served the evening meal.

With a head blow, Émile knocked out Foo.

During suppertime, Didier, a sore loser, objected to the referee's decision. He claimed Émile legally won the fight by knockout and refused to pay off his loss to Germé. First, they argued. Germé called Didier a "stupid, tall giraffe," and Didier called Germé, "idiot; barrel-chested red gorilla." Then Germé punched Didier's face and a fight started. The crew had pleaded with Didier to comply with the referee's decision because he followed the rule and the condition previously set by the captain. Captain Colon intervened and ordered Didier to pay off his loss to Germé because Émile knocked out Foo with a hard head blow. Reluctantly, Didier paid up.

The next morning after breakfast, Didier went to the windward bulwark. (Windward is the side where the wind is blowing from). He urinated upwind over the bulwark, so the wind took the urine and sprayed it all over the boatswain, the referee who disqualified Émile. Then Didier yelled, "Hey, you filthy, stupid puppet. How does that hot shower feel?" That did it. The enraged boatswain jumped all over Didier, flipped him onto the deck, and smashed his face with his foot. When Monsieur De Montaigne tried to separate them, they threw him vigorously on the deck. Upon being separated, Didier discovered he had two black eyes, a bleeding mouth and a broken tooth.

Captain Colon brought both men to Captain Léopold and charged them with fighting aboard the ship. Captain Léopold reprimanded them and took disciplinary actions against both by having their offenses entered in the ship's official logbook and later in their service records. The official logbook would be returned to the marine administrator, a naval officer in charge of this branch of the Merchant Marine. Thereafter, Captain Léopold banned all boxing and gambling on board the ship.

The following morning, Monsieur De Montaigne, the chief engineer, did not show up for breakfast, and later he was found dead in his bed. We assumed he had had a heart attack. Immediately, Captain Colon ordered *"la mise en berne du pavillon."* — (the flag at half-staff). We hoisted the French flag at full halyard and lowered it to half-staff. Monsieur De Montaigne was fifty, medium-sized, and light-complexioned with a pleasant face. He was well-liked and respected by everyone on board. I enjoyed working with him; he was patient with me, and he also helped and encouraged me with my studies. It hurt me to see him dead. I really lost a good friend; I cried over his death until his burial, which was scheduled at 1600 hours that day. The fighters, Germé and Didier, cried while they constructed the canvas bag used for the burial.

During the inventory of Monsieur De Montaigne's personal belongings, we discovered he was a former lieutenant commander in the French Navy. For his funeral, we dressed him in his uniform for a naval officer's burial at sea. Then we placed the body inside the canvas bag, along with leads taken from the ship's ballast that would let the body sink quickly to the bottom of the sea. After the boatswain sewed the bag closed, he placed it over a long board and covered it with a large French flag—the burial flag.

At 1530 hours, Captain Léopold stopped the ship and ordered all hands on deck on the starboard side for the last rite and burial of Lieutenant Commander De Montaigne. Foo and Émile arrived on deck carrying the body and placed it across the bulwark's railing. I blew the Navy's whistle for saluting the arrival of a naval officer. The crew stood at attention while Captain Léopold read the ritual funeral ceremony, ending with the final statement: *"Que les flots recoivent le corps du Lieutenant Commandant De Montaigne enterré avec les honneurs dus a son rang: ansi soit-il."* (We now commit the body of Lieutenant Commander De Montaigne into the depths, buried at sea with due honors to his ranks, amen.) Then the captain gave the order: *"Immerger."* (Immerse). The body was immersed; at once, I blew the Navy's whistle to render the honors. Three gunshots and three short blasts on the ship's whistle followed, and the flag was hoisted to topmost. After Émile released the body and tilted the burial board, the body plunged immediately into the depths, and only the burial board and flag remained on board. I was not the only one crying; everyone on board cried goodbye to a good shipmate.

Lieutenant Commander DeMontaiene's burial at sea

The ship continued on her way to Canada, and Captain Colon made the proper official logbook entry: latitude, longitude, day, time and year that the body of Lieutenant Commander De Montaigne was buried at sea with due military honors.

After the burial, the evening became overcast, and the wind veered around from southwest to northeast. ("Veered around" means the wind changed direction in a clockwise manner). After a while, besides cooling us off, the northeast wind increased to storm velocity, accompanied alternately with thunderstorms. Captain Colon ordered all hands on deck to reduce the sail's area to storm sails. A fine mist of snow commenced, partially reducing our visibility.

During that night following Monsieur De Montaigne's burial, we observed around the ship's masts and rigging the phenomenon of "Saint Elmo's fire." Saint Elmo is considered the patron saint of Mediterranean sailors. Saint Elmo's fire occurs during thunderstorms or when electrified clouds are present. It is the glow which is seen around ship's masts, rigging, or other objects onboard, and it is visible only during complete darkness. The crew interpreted the sight of "Saint Elmo's fire" as a message from Monsieur De Montaigne, saying that all was shipshape with God, and as everyone knew, old sailors never die; they simply fade away. Of course, the crew watched this rare sight in memory of our departed, beloved shipmate. In the morning, just before dawn, the Saint Elmo's fire faded away with the old sailor, Monsieur De Montaigne.

As we continued our voyage, we anticipated encountering "Icebergs" from Greenland's lower glacier. They are carried by the wind and the Labrador Current into the North Atlantic Ocean. Only about one seventh to one tenth of the iceberg's total mass is above water; the top melts away faster, leaving the bottom hidden beneath the surface, which becomes extremely dangerous to ships. The greatest numbers of icebergs reach the ship's route in April, May, and June. "Growlers" are parts of the iceberg that break off and are more or less the size of an average house. They are called growlers because of the noise they make as they float in the waves and grind against each other.

We reached the position where we changed our course in order to cross only the narrowest path of the icebergs and make landfall at Belle Isle, north of Newfoundland. Thereafter, the sea temperature dropped considerably, telling us we were already in the Labrador Current and entering the iceberg's possible path; then our position confirmed that fact. Captain Colon doubled the lookout watches for icebergs, which must be maintained around the clock. One lookout was on the crow's nest, the other on the forecastle deck. Both were equipped with binoculars.

Since we entered the Labrador Current, the water temperature remained constant for the next couple of days. However, we had good visibility because of the northeast wind. In addition, the moonlight added to our night visibility. We continued our course, making good speed, until the wind changed to southwest causing us to lose our good visibility. To add to our anxiety, the water temperature dropped further, and the warmer south wind caused a thick fog to set in. Moreover, we were without radar!

Captain Colon called all hands on deck to secure the

sails. We continued our navigation using the engine only, for we did not want the sails to hinder our maneuverability in the event of an emergency. At that moment, we were in the middle of the icebergs' path. Although we knew the position of most of the icebergs via radio, Captain Léopold would not take the chance of colliding with one; he adjusted our speed to cross the path and to make landfall during daylight.

Suddenly the crow's nest lookout yelled, "I hear growlers! I hear growlers on the port bow!"

Some of the crew panicked, came out on deck, and searched for icebergs, but no one could hear a growler from the deck because of the engine noise. Captain Léopold noted the panicked crew and foresaw the confusion they could create, so he ordered all hands below deck, except those on watch. Meanwhile, Captain Colon stopped the engine and raised only those sails that would not impede our maneuverability.

Again the crow's nest lookout screamed: "Iceberg! Iceberg on the starboard bow!" But the iceberg could not be seen on deck. The crow's nest lookout yelled again: "I see the iceberg's peak above the fog! I can see the iceberg's peak above the low fog bank!"

Captain Léopold asked the lookout, "Germé, tell me precisely how many points off the starboard bow?" (From the bow to the beam are eight points, or 90 degrees; 8 into 90 makes 11.25 degrees, or one point).

Germé answered, "Two points! Two points off the starboard bow, captain!"

Immediately, Captain Léopold ordered hard right rudder, and the southwest wind automatically swung the sails and boom to the starboard side. Without the engine noise, we heard the growlers, and later we saw the iceberg off the port beam, (the beam is at a right angle to the ship's keel) a really big one, as big as a tall mountain. Then we saw the growlers—three of them, the size of one-and two-story houses.

Amazingly, the growlers were all south of the iceberg. Captain Colon explained that the iceberg and its growlers were drifting south with the current from Labrador and were not affected by the weak south wind, so he expected the growlers to be on the south side of the iceberg. Surely that explained Captain Léopold's wise decision to pass on the north side of the iceberg. That hard right rudder saved our lives. If we had hit this iceberg, we could all have died from hypothermia; we had escaped the same accident which caused the *Titanic*'s disaster.

That afternoon, the wind changed to northwest, which lifted the low fog and improved our visibility. We set all sails up and the engine full ahead in an attempt to make landfall before sunset. Just before 1600 hours, the crow's nest and the deck lookout yelled together, "Land ho! Land ho!" Finally, we sighted Belle Isle and Newfoundland, Canada. Some of the men happily yelled, "Yippee! Yippee, we made it! We made it!" Captain

Léopold decided that we had had enough excitement during the long North Atlantic crossing. He chose to anchor the ship for the night, so we could enjoy a peaceful night resting and sleeping.

We spent the night at a safe anchorage near Belle Isle, north of Newfoundland. At sunrise, we picked up the anchor and adjusted our speed to arrive during daylight. Wind and weather permitted, so we navigated for two days around the west coast of Newfoundland and arrived before noon in Saint Pierre, a French territory. The French authority greeted us cordially and welcomed us. The ship docked immediately, and the crew took off into town to celebrate a dangerous but successful North Atlantic crossing.

Iceberg:
We had escaped the same accident which caused the
"Titanic" disaster.

The ship docked immediately and the crew took off
into town to celebrate a successful and dangerous
North Atlantic crossing.

VOYAGE VI

GUSTAVIA

After facing the North Atlantic's most perilous elements without radar, *Putnick*, a square-rigged sailing vessel, escaped the same accident which had caused the Titanic disaster. . Her crewmembers celebrated their triumphant crossing of the treacherous North Atlantic via Iceland from France to Canada. As the *mousse*, the deck boy, I was officially a crewmember. The Saint Pierre Miquelon Association of Fishermen honored *Putnick*'s crew and granted us full membership, which would ensure our use of the local fishermen's facilities.

Following minor repairs and the installation of radar, *Putnick* was ready for a try in a new fishing ground, the Grand Banks of Newfoundland. Our first fishing voyage was well-rewarded with a huge and easy catch. After a few productive fishing voyages, we soon found that the low prices for our catches did not fully cover our expenses. Most fish warehouses were full of frozen and salted fish. The low price forced us to search for a new market for our catches. Unfortunately, we persisted too long in working without totally covering our expenses.

Now, a quick fix was an obvious necessity. The only positive option was to reduce the crew, but we voted unanimously against that. These crises made us discover that we were not only good shipmates, but also a well-adjusted and loving family.

We were broke and unable to pay the ship's operating cost, but the crew held on, working without their shares. Then they found out that the ship might be auctioned for late mortgage payments. In a desperate move to reduce the crew and save *Putnick*, some of the crewmembers volunteered to separate themselves from *Putnick*: Captain Colon took command of the *Désirée*, another vessel, with a full load of frozen and salted fish. (Monsieur Carméné, my old-time friend and now the ship's carpenter; Monsieur Charlo, the boatswain; Germé, Didier, and Bêbert; and Émile, my old-time friend and boxing rival, joined Captain Colon's crew and returned to German-occupied France.) As the ship that took away our brothers backed slowly out of the harbor, we sadly told them goodbye. We would miss them dearly, but we realized they were homesick; also, the financial gain helped us to accept our separation.

Subsequently, Monsieur Levesque was promoted to boatswain, and I replaced Émile in the galley working with Foo. We sailed to the fishing ground, and within a short time, we had a full load of fish. Upon returning to port, the crew pooled all of their savings to pay for the sea store, food, and fuel necessary for a voyage to the French Antilles. Captain Léopold had negotiated a profitable price for our frozen fish. In addition, barrels of salted codfish were crated and lashed on deck. *Putnick* was loaded down to her plimsoll mark (her maximum permitted loading mark).

Salted codfish was an important staple in the Caribbean Islands, because at this time most houses were without refrigeration.

The southbound voyage that started in Iceland resumed, but this time we headed for the Paradise Islands of the Caribbean. During this beautiful voyage, the weather gradually changed from a thick fog and a solid gray sky to a blue sky with a few fluffy white clouds. The sun seemed like a gigantic star, with beams of light radiating from behind the clouds as if they were Heaven's lights. The sea changed from green to indigo blue as we entered the Sargasso Sea, where masses of seaweed float. Then we observed a spectacular sight: the "Phosphorescence of the sea." While the ship moved and pitched, the waves created at the bow and the stern became illuminated by a bluish glow in the dark night. This was due to the presence of various microscopic phosphorescent vegetable and animal life, which shone in the dark when agitated.

As we continued southward, the air temperature warmed, so we peeled off our winter clothes. Wearing only shorts, we bathed in the fresh breeze and the warm sun. The sky, the sea, and the horizon were in perfect harmony and at their best, and a full moon was visible—even the elements welcomed us into the Caribbean Paradise. We saw schools of flying fish, airborne, escaping from sharks, tunas, and whales.

That evening, the horizon was perfect; it allowed us the rare sight of "the sun's green flash." At sea, the horizon line meets

As the *Désirée* backed out slowly with our brothers, we sadly told them goodbye.

with the water line. When the setting sun passes from the clear horizon line into the sea water line, during that brief moment, it is seen as a sudden green flash.

Because there were so many flying fish, we decided to feed on them. We rigged a basket lined with a white sheet and shined a floodlight on it, and, attracted by the light and the white sheet, the flying fish simply flew into the basket. Within a short time, we had baskets full of them. Flying fish are used chiefly for bait, but they are also a delicacy when marinated and fried crisply. They were tasty with our wine; in fact, that evening meal turned out to be a real feast.

As previously mentioned the *Putnick* was a wooden sailing vessel. Naval patrollers's radar or sonar equipment might not detect the vessel, except or visual during the days, nighttime *Putnick* navigated under cover, without lights. Additionally, we took full advantage of the trade wind and favorable current for best possible speed.

Early the following morning, we arrived at Saint Barthelemy, a small, isolated island far away from, yet legally part of, Guadeloupe. Her beautiful harbor, with its crystal clear blue water, showed her sandy, rocky bottom and reflected her blue sky with snow-white scattered clouds. The air temperature was around 80 degrees, and the light breeze that caressed my skin felt good, so unlike the frozen, gray weather we had just left behind in Iceland and Newfoundland. The sight of a paved side of one of her dominant hills surprised me; I found out it was used to collect rainwater because this area had not enough fresh water. Another unusual sight along the sides of the few roads were pigs, goats, and lambs tied there to pasture. That evening and the following one, the crew celebrated its arrival in Gustavia, a former Danish settlement. The people, most of Danish descent, were tall, slim, sun-tanned, and beautiful, and they welcomed us eagerly.

Finally, we unloaded our salted and frozen cargo and

stored the ship for sea with fuel, food, and whatever was available to us. While no one was looking, we borrowed and froze a few of their pigs, goats, and lambs and set sail for the return trip to Saint Pierre, Newfoundland. The crew had a good time, and as an old sailor's tall tale went after a good port, the crew said, "We won the battle of Gustavia." If any shipmate had been left behind in jail, the hospital, or the cemetery, we would have lost the battle of Gustavia.

Until now, the return voyage had been without incident, except for the change in our menus. We took a vacation from our thrice-daily fish, enjoying instead pork, lamb, and goat meat. As we sailed northward from Bermuda, we passed through one of Cape Hatteras' storms and lost our top jib's halyard. This forward jib sail was necessary for the ship to "go about": that is, to go on the opposite tack, turning the ship's head on the opposite side of the wind when sailing upwind. After the storm, someone had to shin up the topsail mast and pass a heaving line, a thin line, through the halyard's block. This heaving line would be spliced to a new halyard and hove through the jib's block.

Because Émile was gone, I was the only one who might be able to shin up the topsail mast. After some thought, I remembered Captain Léopold's order to be a brave *mousse*, so I volunteered to do this difficult task above four stepped parts of the forward mast! Giving me much advice about how to do it, the boatswain carried the heaving line and accompanied me up the first three sets of ratlines—steps or a rope ladder rigged between the mast's shrouds and used to go up the mast. We climbed up to the crosstree at the foot of the topmost mast. The boatswain made a loop with a bowknot that had a tail longer than the top sail's mast; he passed the loop over my head and around my neck, so that the bowknot hung over my back and the end of the long tail was attached with a slipknot. That rigging allowed me to tow the heaving line while shinning up the mast. Then the boatswain said, "*Mousse*, you must do exactly as I order you. That is very important to our success."

"Yes, bosun."

"Now start climbing."

"Yes, bosun."

When I had shinned halfway up the topmost mast, the boatswain noticed that I was tired and ordered me to stop climbing: "Stop, stop, *Mousse*. Hold on firmly. Close your eyes. Do not look down. Now rest for a while, and do not look down."

But I had just taken a look down, and I saw the ship's small outline about 135 feet below, and the blue ocean covered with white crested swells. As the ship rolled without sails, the topmost mast swung, with me on it, well clear of the ship's deck... way off over the water. I felt exhausted and unable to continue shinning, but I held on tightly to the mast and yelled, "*Oh, mon Dieu.*" (Oh, my God). I thought of letting myself drop into the water at the next swing of the topmast. But the boatswain kept on saying, "Hold on Joe-Joe, hold on, close your eyes and rest for a while; I am with you and remember you must do exactly as I order you. "

"Yes, bosun."

"Now, Joe-Joe, open your eyes and start climbing."

I did, and reached the top. Then the boatswain said, "Joe-Joe, pass the long tail end of the heaving line through the block; release the slipknot and lower the end to me."

"Yes, bosun."

"Now take the loop off your neck and slide down slowly until you reach me."

"Yes, bosun."

I did as the boatswain instructed.

When we returned on deck, Captain Léopold said, "*Mousse*, I knew you could do it and I am proud of you." Then the captain added, "You have now proven that you are able, and there is nothing to fear but your own negative thoughts, so I want you to be more positive in everything you do, and that is an order."

"Yes, sir."

The boatswain and everyone else congratulated me for my courage and bravery, but what about the boost of courage the boatswain gave me? I am positive that I would not have successfully completed this difficult task without the boatswain's support and instructions. Meanwhile, Monsieur Charlec spliced the end of the heaving line to a new jib's halyard and passed it through the jib's head block. Then the crew heaved up all the sails and headed the ship as close as possible into the northerly wind, so now she changed her tack more quickly when necessary.

The weather improved, and we made good headway to the north until Sable Island was on the port beam; actually, we had reached the Grand Bank of Newfoundland. The wind changed to the southwest, so we encountered the usual thick fog that forced us to reduce our speed. We had to keep a sharp lookout to avoid icebergs and other vessels; nevertheless, we docked before sunset in Saint Pierre, off Newfoundland.

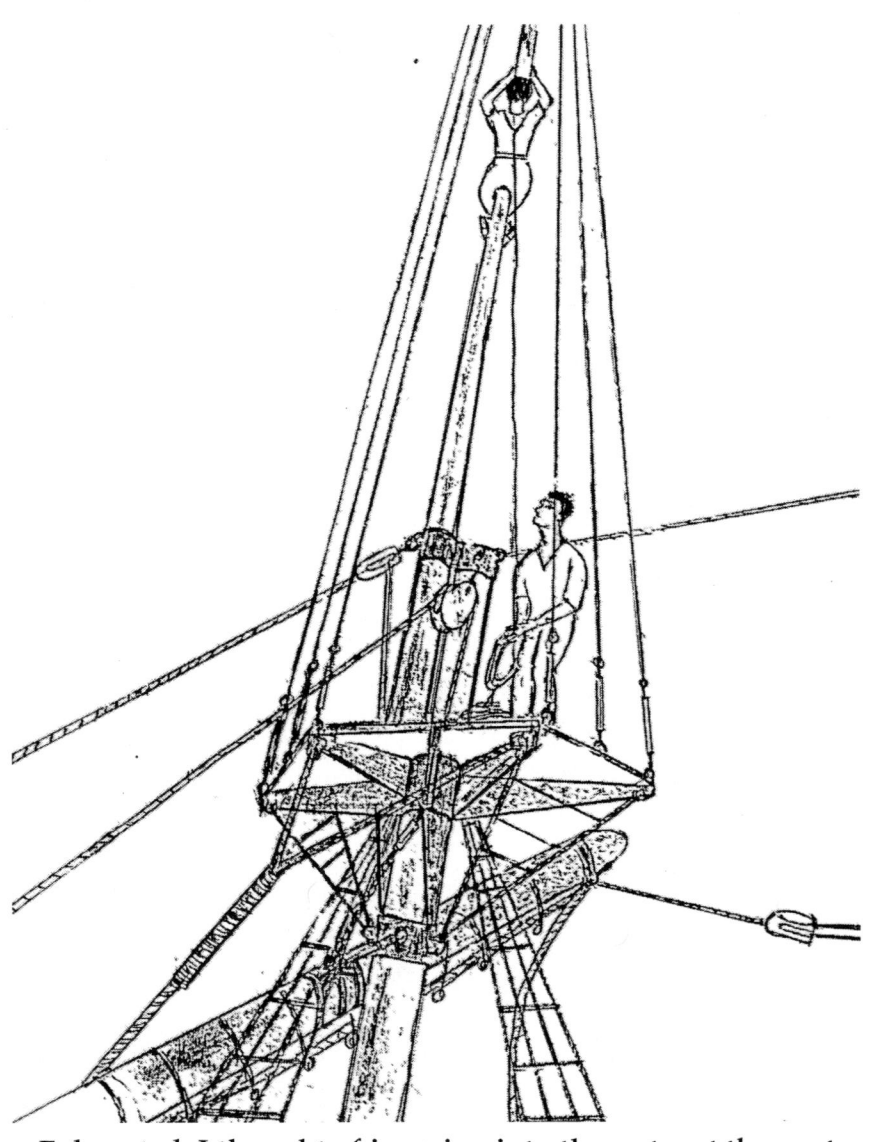

Exhausted, I thought of jumping into the water at the next swing of the mast.

VOYAGE VII
THE PIGERMEN

We fished on the Grand Bank of Newfoundland and sold the fish in the French Antilles. On this particular voyage, we cleaned and painted *Putnick's* bottom; she would now make better speed. Because it was too hot to cook below deck in the tropics, we constructed a galley on the open deck.

In Saint Pierre and Miquelon, the surplus of frozen and salted fish increased beyond belief. That made it possible for the owner, Captain Léopold, to purchase at an auction a shipload of frozen and salted codfish at a great savings. So at a bargain price, we quickly loaded someone else's fish and sailed back to Saint Barthelemy in the Caribbean. A strong northeast wind favored us, so we made good speed toward the south. We rapidly left behind the gray, cold weather of Newfoundland and began to enjoy spring-like weather. We also had bought chicken, beef, and pork to alter our usual fish menu. With the good weather, we were happy to be alive.

I was still working with Foo in the galley. One morning, Foo told me to peel potatoes and to put them in a large pot, half-filled with water. When this large pot was filled with potatoes, Foo and I wanted to lift the pot and put it on top of the stove. I failed to lift the pot all the way up on top of the stove; Foo got angry with me for being unable to lift the pot. He shoved me, and I fell into the garbage can with my butt first, so my thigh and my back got locked into the garbage can. Then the ship rolled, and the can fell on its side with me locked in and rolled to the corner of the galley. Foo laughed and laughed at me while saying, "The garbage is stuck into the garbage can where it belongs." Finally, I freed myself from the garbage can and got up on my feet.

**Then the ship rolled and the can fell on its side,
rolling to the corner of the Galley.**

Enraged, I grabbed Foo, raised him up and put him on top of the hot stove; he yelled like a pig. Everyone rushed to the galley to investigate what happened. Foo was badly burned, so Captain Léopold treated his burns.

Then the captain questioned both of us about what happened. Foo first explained to the captain exactly what happened, the truth. But I defended myself and told the captain: "Foo, an amateur boxer, punched me and knocked me out into the garbage can, and I got stuck in it. Foo laughed and laughed, saying the garbage belonged in the garbage can." The captain reprimanded both of us for fighting on board the ship. Because of his burn, Foo was placed off duty until arrival in Gustavia. Furthermore, the captain ordered me to continue the cooking all day without any help, and he added, "The food better be good and ready on time." Although Foo often passed by the galley and glared at me, the voyage continued without further incidents between us, and no one complained about my cooking either!

In the early morning, we finally arrived in Gustavia and dropped both anchors. Immediately, the Port Authority arrived and cleared the ship. The stevedores commenced discharging our cargo into refrigerated barges and scows. Afterward, without any explanation, the Authority informed us that the crew, except for the captain, was denied shore liberty for the duration of the port time. No one demanded an explanation because we knew that on the last trip, without permission, we had taken a few of their grazing animals. Without interruption, the cargo discharging continued until 5 PM.

In the morning at 5 AM, one of my duties was to light the coal stove in the galley; I also made fresh coffee, biscuits, and preparations for breakfast. The boatswain usually was up first and drank his coffee early, but this particular morning, he was busy preparing heaving line and fishing hook; although the coffee was ready, he had not had any yet. Then the boatswain approached the galley door while looking at the beach through binoculars, and said, *"Il est gros et beau."* (He is big and beautiful.) He repeated this remark until I asked him, *"Quoi?"* (What?) He handed me the binoculars and said, *"Regarde."* (Look.) On the beach, I saw a big, white pig, which seemed to be about 200 pounds. I said, "Yes, he is big and beautiful." I returned the binoculars to him.

"It is too bad you are chicken."

"Me, chicken! Why?"

"If you were not chicken, we could take this big pig."

"How?"

"You could swim to the beach and bring the pig a baited hook."

"Oh, yes, what about all the sharks?"

"You see, you are yellow."

With the boatswain's binoculars, I saw the big, white
pig on the beach.

The boatswain kept on going away from me while holding his pipe and puffing smoke. He irked me by calling me chicken and yellow. I ran after him beating my chest, and said, "I am not chicken nor yellow."

"*Je le savais.*" (I knew it.)

Before having his coffee, the boatswain had prepared his heaving line with a loop that had a tail attached to a baited fishing hook wrapped in a towel to protect me from the hook. He had prepared all these and expected to use them on me! The boatswain quickly grabbed the loop and passed it over my head and around my neck; such rigging allowed me to swim and tow the heaving line with the fishing hook. Then he pointed to the pig and said, "*Aller à toute vitesse.*" (Go at full speed.) The boatswain also knew that I was a good swimmer.

I dived from the bulwark rail and arrived near the pig rapidly. The pig must have been a pet; he approached me and rubbed his body against my legs while purring contentedly. I scratched his belly to make him feel at home; next, I removed the towel around the baited hook and gave it to the pig. He snapped at the big piece of meat. When the hook spiked him, the pig screamed so loud that he scared me. I ran, dived, and disappeared under water for a while.

When I surfaced, the pig passed me like a speedboat; the boatswain was pulling him toward the ship as fast as he could. The pig's owner heard the screaming and squealing. When he investigated, he saw his pig and me swimming toward the

Through his binoculars, the boatswain saw the friendly pig; I scratched his belly and he purred contentedly.

ship. He ran for his rifle and started shooting at me; I dived deeply and zigzagged under water before surfacing for breath. Lucky for me, he had to reload after each bullet, which gave me a chance; he did not know exactly where I was and where I would surface for air. The rifle noise, the pig and I swimming, the pig squealing and bleeding, all these disturbances in the water, and especially the blood, attracted the sharks.

When the boatswain saw the sharks, he panicked and called the captain. "Captain, Captain Léopold, come quickly with your rifles; many sharks are going to eat our Joe-Joe, the *mousse*." Captain Léopold started shooting at the sharks to get them away from me. At the same time, the pig's owner was shooting at my black head of hair each time I surfaced for air. Now, I had to dodge bullets from two different directions; the captain could easily mistake my black head for a shark's black dorsal fin. I was in a lot of trouble, and the sharks tripled my danger. The pig arrived along the side of the ship ahead of me; with one of the captain's rifles, the boatswain put a bullet into the pig's head. All this commotion awoke the crew before time, so all hands were on deck. Using a tackle, some of the crew heaved up the 200 pound pig and quickly buried it well below the ice in one of the freezer compartments. Meanwhile the boatswain and other members of the crew threw me a ring buoy and pulled me up on deck. On my way up, I felt my foot touch one of the sharks. Standing on the deck, I realized the bullets and sharks had missed me, so I yelled, "Yippee!"

Right after that, the *"gendarmes"* (police) arrived on board and said to the boatswain, "The crew stole a pig with a fishing line."

"You mean they fished a pig."

"Yes."

"That is not possible; we are fishermen, not pigermen."

"We want to search the ship."

"Sir, you must first speak with the captain."

The captain welcomed the police and agreed for them to search his ship. Of course, the police could not find any pig because they were afraid to go inside all of the freezer compartments; it was hot outside compared to below zero degrees in the freezer compartments. They opened the door of the compartment that contained the pig and backed out; if they had scratched the ice, they would have seen the pig. The police apologized to the captain and left the ship.

The stevedores completed the cargo discharging at 10 AM. Immediately, we sailed away from Gustavia and removed the pig from the freezer. On this voyage, the natives were not so naïve as on the last trip; they were not eager to welcome us. Now, we were denied shore liberty, the police nearly jailed us, and sharks and bullets nearly killed our *mousse*, so, as the old sailor's tall tale would have said after a port, "The battle of Gustavia was nearly lost, but it was a draw! If any shipmate were left behind

The pig arrived along the side of the ship ahead of me.

in jail, in the hospital, or in the cemetery, we would have lost the battle of Gustavia." After dinner, the boatswain called all hands on deck for sails' rigging. With the wind abaft the beam (beam is at right angle with ship's keel), we heaved up all the sails including the large flying jib. The elements were right for us, and *Putnick* was making good speed toward the north, heading for Newfoundland. The crew started to clean the 200 pound pig. Using hot water from the distillation tank, they scraped and washed the pig.

Monsieur Étienne knew how to cut meat, and we packed the meat for the freezer. Then at suppertime, we had fresh pan-fried pork chops; they were delicious. The following day Monsieur Étienne made sausage, *pâté de campagne*, meat pie, headcheese, and for dinner, he roasted a ham. The following few days, especially to tease us, each time one of the crew passed near the boatswain or me, he squealed like a pig; they also called us the pigermen because we had done the unheard of—pig fishing!

Although the visibility was good, we reduced our speed by lowering the sails that would encumber our maneuverability.

For the next five days, we made good time toward the north. The wind and current both stayed abaft the beam, and we had a strong southerly wind. The weather stayed clear and beautiful; then Sable Island appeared on the starboard beam. Although the visibility was good, we reduced our speed by lowering the sails that would encumber our maneuverability; we had to avoid many icebergs and other vessels. However, the following morning, we arrived in Saint Pierre. The crew was happy; they had money; Captain Léopold had given them a draw, and they ran ashore to celebrate the end of a beautiful and lively voyage.

We are fisherman, not pigermen.

VOYAGE VIII
POINTE-À-PITRE

Following our arrival in Saint Pierre, the Port Authority told us that a French troller, *Le Breton*, recently had arrived from France, and they confirmed that the *Désirée*, Captain Colon's ship, had arrived in Cherbourg, France; the ship, crew, and the cargo were in good condition.

That evening, our crew had another good reason for celebrating the good news from Captain Colon and his crew. During these festivities, a brawl broke out between the natives and our crew, which caused an altercation between us and the police. Nearly half of our crew was jailed; Captain Léopold had to pay fifty francs ($10.00) fine per man for their release, which was an expensive experience. So, as the old sailor's tall tale would have gone, "We lost the battle of Saint Pierre, because half of our crew was jailed, and we disgraced our home port."

The political situation had changed in Saint Pierre and Miquelon; the people no longer were loyal to the French government. The surplus of frozen and salted fish was no longer for sale or bargain; fishermen were holding onto their catches, expecting to sell for a much higher price. Captain Léopold and the crew decided on storing the ship for sea and sailed to the Grand Bank to fish for our own market.

After approximately two weeks of fishing, our freezers were filled. We did not return to Saint Pierre, but went instead to Saint Johns, Newfoundland. We picked up, at a bargain price, a load of salted pork in barrels. During this time, salted pork was an important staple in the Caribbean Islands, again because of the lack of refrigeration.

In Saint Johns, we filled the below deck galley with the barrels of salted pork. We loaded, crated, and lashed barrels all over the deck and constructed another deck over them. Also, we erected safety wire and rail all around the deck. Extension wires were installed to the deck's pad eyes for securing the sails' rigging. *Putnick* had a bigger load than on the last voyage. After taking on fresh provisions, fuel and water, she was deeply loaded down, and we sailed for Pointe-à-Pitre, Guadeloupe, French Antilles.

The voyage started well with a strong northerly wind. We made as much way as possible to the south, looking for warmer weather. After we passed Bermuda, the wind shifted to southerly, causing us to sail upwind, tacking (The ship is run with the wind on each side of the bow for an equal distance when possible.) We were happy as long as the ship made southerly way. The crossing continued normally. The flying fish were again airborne, fleeing predators; we decided to feed on them as well.

We progressed southward normally until we were north of the Virgin Islands. We knew about a small tropical disturbance there, and we prepared to meet it. All sails were secured, and to reduce the ship's rolling, a couple of storm sails were rigged. This "small disturbance" turned out to be much more dangerous than predicted. Using the engine only, we continued on our way as the wind and swells increased. Captain Léopold ordered the safety wire to be stretched and instructed the crew, when required to be on deck, to use their safety belts. (The safety belt's hook slides on the safety wire, preventing the sailor from being washed overboard by heavy sea.) Then the swells became dangerously high. *Putnick* rose above one swell and dove into a trough as deep as the previous swell. Sea and swells rolled toward us and crashed over the deck cargo.

The vessel was "hove to" (The vessel's way is checked or is held with no way rising and falling with the sea and swells). Captain Léopold changed his course to escape the storm and its heavy swells. The sea calmed as we fled, and we were doing well until a heavy swell caused the ship to snap roll and parted the forward topmost mast. Then the sea grabbed the broken piece of mast and tore off the chain plates (Chain plates are metal strips secured to the side of the ship to which the lower end of the mast's shroud is fastened. The shroud is one of a set of wires which are extended on each side of the masthead to the side of the ship to support the mast up, laterally). The weather cleared considerably, but we were taking on water rapidly. Even the engine room's two pumps plus the two hand-operated pumps on deck could not hold back the incoming water.

Captain Léopold decided to rig a collision mat. The mat is made of two thicknesses of the heaviest canvas, and is used to temporarily stop the inrush of water through an accidental opening in the hull. Of the four corners of the mat, two corners are attached to the forward and the after lines, and the other two are attached to the upper and the lower hugging lines. The lower hugging line must be passed under the ship's bottom and up on the opposite side. Someone must dive under the ship's bottom.

Since I was the best diver, I agreed to dive underneath the ship in a rough sea. I listened to everyone's advice. The boatswain and I got into the dinghy, and he passed around my neck a heaving line loop, made with a bowline knot, that freed both of my hands for swimming. Then he said, "Joe-Joe, dive deep enough to avoid the ship's bottom and swim rapidly." I dived and swam as fast as I could, but the location of the damaged hull was too deep in the water. I could not complete the crossing under the ship, and because I needed air badly, I returned—but rose too fast for a breath of air. The ship moved down toward me, and I bumped against its bottom so barnacles ripped at my back. (Barnacles are marine fouling which become attached to the ship's bottom; their shells are razor sharp). When I surfaced, Captain Léopold noticed that I was bleeding, so he ordered me to return on deck. The captain treated the barnacle cuts and had me put on a tight, long-sleeved shirt to protect me against additional cuts. Then he chose a location forward of the damaged hull, less deep and less wide; this location would make it easier for me to complete the dive and pass the heaving line underneath the moving ship's bottom.

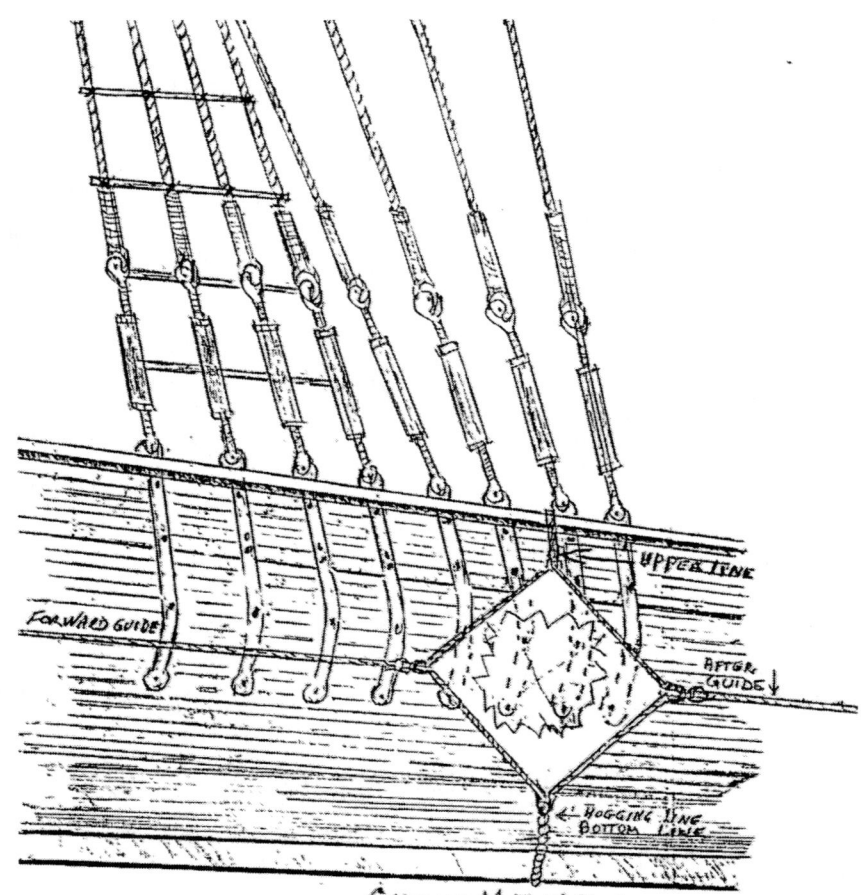

Collision Mat in Place
Over the Damaged Chaine Plate.

The boatswain waited for me with his looped heaving line; he passed it again over my head and around my neck and said, "Joe-Joe, this time swim faster, keep your eyes open and look out for the ship's bottom. I will be on the other side, waiting for you in the dinghy."

Captain Léopold said, "Joe-Joe, this dive is our last chance, and we are sinking fast." I dived and swam as fast as I could, with my eyes open as the boatswain had recommended. I looked up and saw the ship's bottom coming down on me; I quickly dived deeper, and it missed me. I swam faster and I saw the dinghy's bottom. I knew I was almost on the other side of the ship. I ran out of breath, but I forced myself to swim faster for a little more. I started to rise as I swam, but I came up too fast, and I was a little short of reaching the dinghy. On my way up, my body and head dragged against the ship's hull that moved up and down on me; its barnacles cut me several times as I sought desperately to surface for a breath of air. Finally, I surfaced, and the boatswain grabbed me and pulled me up into the dinghy. He quickly turned me over, opened my mouth, and checked to see if I was breathing. Then he hugged me, saying, "*Dieu, merci, il est vivant.*" (Thank God, he is alive.) The crew pulled me up on deck. I tried to look tough, but the salt water over those multiple cuts burned me for hours. The captain treated all the cuts that I had received. Then he said, "You are in good shape; I will look at you tomorrow."

"Thank you, sir."

Meanwhile, the boatswain and his crew attached three heavy shackles around the heaving line; one on each side of the ship, and one in the middle to keep the line away from the ship's hull. Then they pulled the heaving line under the ship until it reached the damaged part of the hull. By the time Captain Léopold completed the treatment of my barnacle cuts, the boatswain and his crew had installed the collision mat. The inrush of water was under control, and only the engine room's two pumps continued pumping. The crew took a break from the manual pumps and the bucket brigade. Then they picked up the broken piece of the mast and lashed it on the deck. The weather calmed; we heaved up all the sail that could be rigged on the remainder of the ship's masts and got underway again. Except for those on sea watches, everyone returned to his routine duties.

In the morning, Captain Léopold removed all the bandages from my wounds; they were dried out and red. The captain said, "I will check them out daily until they are healed." He also added, "You stay off duty for a couple of days." Believe me, I needed the days to recover from those barnacle cuts. I suffered so much; I could not lie down or turn around, and I could not sleep either. The captain had to give me some painkillers because I felt so miserable.

"Joe-Joe, dive deeper this time!"

Years ago, a defiant, uncontrollable sailor would be disciplined by being "Keelhauled." He was tied up with a good line and dragged under the ship's keel, so barnacles could cut him up as punishment; he usually drowned, but occasionally one survived this severe ordeal. After my two diving experiences underneath the ship, I realized that I had been keelhauled twice, but in reverse—I was pulling the line under the ship's keel, rather than the line pulling me under, but the result is the same either way: The sailor ends up cut by barnacles, as I was.

Yet another punishment in the old days was to "walk the plank." A plank was fastened and projected a short distance over the ship's side. Then, blindfolded, the sailor was forced to walk that plank until he fell overboard. So, a defiant sailor could have been "keelhauled," or just dumped overboard.

We continued on our southerly heading, hoping to reach Guadeloupe, but the leakage from our repairs again overcame the engine room's two pumps. We had to start the deck's manual pumps. The ship's speed and motion reduced the effectiveness of the collision mat. Captain Léopold said, "If we could continue the patching to control the incoming water, we could approach a small sand island not too far away and beach the ship in order to make our repairs of the hull."

The following day before sunset, we arrived at the sand island, not far from Guadeloupe. Captain Léopold had all sails secured and ordered the boatswain to standby the starboard anchor. Using the engine only, he carefully approached the beach and headed the ship into the light wind, while I continually reported to him the depth of water under the ship's keel. Then the captain yelled, *"Mouiller."* (Let go.) The boatswain dropped the starboard anchor and yelled, *"One shackle."* (90 feet of chain out). Then he rang the anchor bell once, to report one shackle.

"Hold it."

"Dragging."

"Slack off."

"Two shackles." The boatswain rang the anchor bell twice.

"Holding."

The captain ordered the boatswain to heave on the anchor's chain until one shackle was on the water's edge.

"One shackle." The anchor bell rang once.

"Hold it."

"Holding."

"Secure the anchor, engage the wildcat (a grooved drum which grabs the chain links to raise or lower the anchor) and flip the riding pawl" (a hinged piece of steel that prevents any chain backward motion).

"Anchor secured."

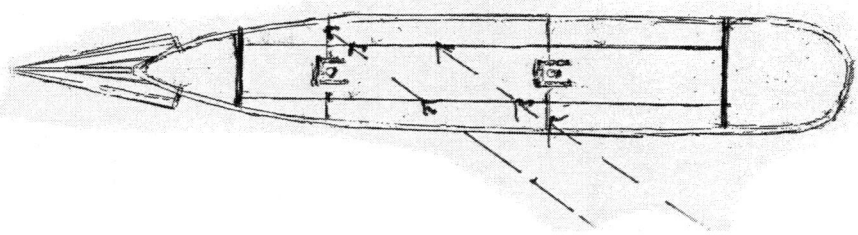

The safety belt's hook slides on *the safety wire*, preventing the sailor from being washed overboard by heavy sea..

The anchor ball was hoisted, the anchor's lights were rigged on the bow and the stern; other navigation lights were turned off, and all deck lights were lit. Because the ship made no way, the collision mat adhered more to the hull and reduced the incoming water, and the engine room's pumps continued to work. During the night, the anchor watches carefully checked the ship's position and how the anchor was holding. If in doubt, they would call the captain immediately. In the morning, the crew would resume the repair.

Using the engine only, he carefully approached
the sandy beach.

VOYAGE VIII A
SAND ISLAND

We spent the night at anchor with one shackle of chain out and at the water's edge. During the night, however, the anchor held well to the sandy bottom. At sunrise, the captain ordered all hands on deck. Then he ordered the boatswain to stand by on the bow's starboard anchor and to pay out, or slack, on the starboard anchor chain. Using the engine and the rudder, he maneuvered the ship so that the anchor chain paid out and led directly ahead. The boatswain yelled, "Three shackles." Then he rang the anchor bell three times.

"Hold it."

"Holding." Now, the starboard anchor had a long forward lead with three shackles of chain out.

We carried a spare mushroom anchor secured on the bow. Previously, we had shifted it to the stern on the port side and hung it over the side ready to be dropped; the anchor's ring was attached to a good eight-inch manila hawser with the shackles correctly marked.

With the boatswain standing by the bow anchors and Monsieur Étienne standing by the stern anchor, the captain maneuvered the ship using the engine and the rudder so as to shift the stern away from the beach. Then he yelled, "Stern let go."

Monsieur Étienne dropped the stern port anchor and yelled, "One shackle."

"Hold it."

"Holding."

The captain ordered the boatswain on bow to heave on the anchor chain until the two shackles mark was on deck. At the . same time Monsieur Étienne and Maurice were to slack on the stern anchor hawser until the two shackles mark was on deck.

The boatswain yelled, "Two shackles on deck on the bow."

Monsieur Étienne yelled, "Two shackles on deck on the stern."

"Hold it on the bow, engage the wildcat, the riding pawl, and secure."

"Hold it on the stern and secure."

"Holding on the bow and secured."

"Holding on the stern and secured."

Then the anchor watches continually checked the ship's position and how she rode between the bow and stern anchors.

After breakfast, we started to heel, or tilt, the ship to port sufficiently to raise the opposite damaged side above water. Using the ship's cargo booms and tackle, first we shifted some of the starboard deck cargo to the port side, above the deck cargo already there. Next, we discharged from the starboard deck all the remaining pork barrels and dropped them into the water; they sunk immediately to the bottom. Then we shifted some fuel and water from the starboard side tanks to the port side tanks. The vessel listed to the port side and raised the opposite side above water, so we could properly complete the repairs on the starboard side. We used, in double thickness, some of the best planks that previously secured our deck cargo, and properly caulked them with oakum to seal the hole.

After dinner, Foo and I went to investigate the small sand island; it was covered with sea birds. The island was also stoneless, but there were plenty of birds and turtles' eggs; sea turtles were working among the birds. Since we were fresh out of eggs, we picked a few buckets of the larger sea birds' eggs and some of the turtles'; after we left the island, we ate eggs in every possible way, and a bucket of hard-boiled eggs was always on the stove.

Using a *scoop*, a fish landing net, Foo and I grabbed about a dozen of the larger birds, cut off their heads, and immediately, started to pluck them. The birds were loaded with bugs and lice; they covered us from head to toe. We quickly dived into the sea to remove these harmful pests from our bodies. But the salt water caused them to stick more to our skin.

When we dived in the water, we discovered the sandy bottom was paved with clams. We could take care of the clams later, though; our priorities were to get the lice off our bodies.

Then Foo remembered when he had lice that his mother used to groom his hair with a mixture of vaseline and kerosene. We realized that kerosene is almost the same as diesel fuel, and the ship had tanks full of that. We rapidly returned on board, grabbed some diesel fuel and rubbed each other with it, so the lice and bugs fell off immediately. Our next problem was to remove the diesel fuel and its smell from our bodies, but we would see to that after stocking up.

We returned to the beach with two burlap bags and filled them with clams. We ate fresh raw clams, steamed clams, and made clam broth; a pot of clam broth remained on the stove. The birds were the size of Cornish hens. We roasted them, but the larger birds were also the oldest ones, and their meat was the toughest. That did not stop us from eating them; Foo had to cook them for a second time as chicken and rice, but they did not exactly taste like chicken. We could have tried some of the smaller, younger birds, but we did not want any more of their lice and bugs.

All hands were restricted to complete our repairs, but the following day Foo and I returned to the beach and turned a couple of sea turtles on their backs. First, we chopped off their heads; then using a hatchet and a hand saw, we opened their carcasses to get at their meat. We made turtle soup, turtle stew, and turtle steaks for dinner. Since the turtle meat turned out to be such a delicacy, we returned to the island and gathered more turtles, and froze the meat for later meals.

We finished our flood control repairs, but we could not make our radio work; it had probably gotten too wet. We now had to get the ship on even keel. We shifted the fuel and water back to their proper starboard side tanks, and moved the barrels that were shifted to the port side back to the starboard side; with this, the ship righted herself somewhat. We had also to reload . the barrels that were in the bottom of the sea, but someone would have to dive for them. Foo had to prepare the meal, and the crew would be busy reloading and securing the barrels, so I was elected as diver.

I was not allowed to eat my lunch, because I had to dive. Soon after lunch, the boatswain and I got into the dinghy floating over the barrels; he had the captain's rifle to protect me from sharks or barracudas that might attack me. Then the boatswain said, "Dive, Joe-Joe." Using barrel hooks (two rods fastened to a center ring with a flat hook at each end), I dove most of the afternoon and hooked all the barrels on the bottom of the sea, which were secured on the starboard side deck. With the ship finally on an even keel, we tightened the collision mat over our damaged hull.

That afternoon, we picked up the stern's anchor. Next, we heaved up on the bow's anchor, and the boatswain yelled, "One shackle on deck" then rang the anchor bell once. He next called, "Anchor aweigh" (The anchor is off the bottom), and rang several strokes on the anchor bell.

The captain ordered, "Secure the anchor for sea and lower the anchor ball."

With the engine at full speed, we sailed away from the bountiful, convenient sandy island which had saved us from the ocean's furies. We rigged all the sails that could be rigged, and we had a late supper of delicious turtle steak. The best and biggest steak was reserved for me as compensation for the lunch I missed, but I could not eat it all; it was too big. Of course, the boatswain helped me eat my steak, as he had been doing all along. I had my meals with him, and we had agreed that I would trade my wine ration for all of his desserts and cheese. I also became the boatswain's sidekick. In addition to his seamanship teaching, he added French grammar and mathematics to help the captain with my education.

The following day, we encountered rough sea, and it opened the seams of our damaged hull. In spite of our efforts to control the leakage, the intake of water again overcame the output of the engine room's bilge pumps. Because we could not stop the intake of water, Captain Léopold decided to enter the nearest port, Basse-Terre, Guadeloupe, in lieu of our destination, Pointe-à-Pitre, Guadeloupe.

That afternoon, we arrived in Basse-Terre's harbor and dropped the anchor. A half-hour later, the Port Authority arrived, cleared the ship, and welcomed us. Then the officer said,

"Captain, we thought you encountered the last big storm and your vessel had foundered, and you and your crew were lost at sea."

Saved from the ocean's fury, we sailed away from this bountiful, convenient, sandy island.

"Believe me, we nearly did."

Then the port official explained, "You are more than a week overdue in Pointe-à-Pitre. Unexpectedly, you showed up here. Captain, your ship could be called a ghost ship, because no one has heard from you since you left Newfoundland."

"That is right, we nearly lost the ship; but we surely lost our foremast and the ship's radio."

"Oh, that is why no one heard from your vessel!"

"You can believe it; we are lucky to be here."

"I will inform Pointe-à-Pitre that your vessel just limped into this port."

Captain Léopold went ashore on the Port Authority's motorboat. He contacted his agent and made arrangements for a launch service for the crew's shore liberty. Some of the crew went ashore for a while, except those on anchor and bilge pump watches. The launch service also brought fresh provisions on board.

In the morning, the stevedores commenced unloading our cargo into refrigerated barges and scows, which would be towed to Pointe-à-Pitre. As we unloaded, the ship became lighter and floated upward, so that the damaged side rose above the water. Simultaneously, a barge with shore-side ship's carpenters made temporary repairs to the ship's hull. That evening, we sailed to Pointe-à-Pitre and adjusted our speed to arrive there early in the morning. Upon arrival, we went directly to a shipyard for the proper repairs.

Basse-Terre

Pointe-à-Pitre

VOYAGE IX

TIBURONES

After inclement weather, we arrived in Pointe-à-Pitre, Guadeloupe, with substantial damages. A hull inspection for repair found that the ship required the removal of the fish freezer compartments. During Captain Léopold's search to finance the repair, he learned that a Dominican company wanted a used refrigerated plant. The company agreed on the price, and a bank offered to finance it, but the Dominican Company wanted the refrigerated plant to be delivered in Ciudad Trujillo. So Captain Léopold arranged for the removal of the refrigerated plant and the hull repair to be done by the same shipyard, in Ciudad Trujillo, Santo Domingo.

During our time in Pointe-à-Pitre, Guadeloupe, Monsieur Charlec, the boatswain; Monsieur Étienne, the sailmaker; and Pierrot, the mechanic, were drafted by the French Navy. Foo, my friend and boxing rival, wanted to go to Saigon, his homeland, so he joined a vessel sailing to Saigon, French Indo-China.

The Pointe-à-Pitre's shipyard completed the temporary repairs, and we loaded sea stores for the voyage to Ciudad Trujillo. Captain Léopold hired Monsieur Fernand as boatswain and Monsieur Gobert as mechanic. He also hired Hammed, a drifter from Senegal, as cook. That afternoon, we sailed from

Pointe-à-Pitre to Ciudad Trujillo.

This new crew treated me only as the *mousse*. Not only had I lost most of my friends from the original crew, but I was also no longer anyone's pet.

Without complications, we arrived in the morning in Ciudad Trujillo. On arrival, we temporarily docked at the end of the first dock in the mouth of the Ozama River. An outer breakwater at a right angle to the river's outflow protected the dock. At low tide, *Putnick*'s main deck was about even with the concrete dock. A few bad boys, called the *"Tiburones"* (Sharks), were standing on the dock admiring the rare and beautiful French tall ship. At that time, Captain Léopold was seated under the poop deck's awning and gave a temporary draw of five dollars to each one of the crew, including me.

The boatswain objected, saying, "Captain, the *mousse* should not be entitled to five dollars the same as me, the boatswain."

Then the captain said, *"Mousse*, come back here. Give me the five dollars; here is two dollars." I took the bills and threw them at the captain. The captain said "Insolent," and he slapped my face. I grabbed his hand and bit it hard; he yelled. Then he slapped me a couple of more times; in so doing, he tripped me. As I fell, on my way down, I grabbed his thigh and bit him again. He yelled, *"arrêter."* (stop.)

The new mechanic, Monsieur Gobert, interfered and

stopped the fight; then he said, "Captain, you have no right to strike the *mousse*." The captain answered, "This boy is my adopted son and, as his father, I have every right to correct him for his insolence and disrespect. In addition, he bit me twice."

Meanwhile on the dock, the *Tiburones* were watching, laughing, and clapping their hands; they were enjoying the fight, and they were saying things in Spanish that I did not understand. Enraged, I jumped on the dock and knocked out two of them, so the other two ran away. As an amateur boxer, overcoming them was easy for me. Satisfied with my revenge on the *Tiburones*, I turned around to return to the ship; suddenly, one of them shoved me into the river. I did not know which one of them did the shoving, but I remembered seeing all four of them on the dock pointing their fingers at me and laughing as the rapid current took me downstream.

Immediately, Captain Léopold ordered the emergency crew to launch the motorboat and rescue me, but before they could reach me, I had crash-landed over the outer rock breakwater.

The following day, we shifted to the shipyard, and the removal of the freezer plant commenced. To my surprise, the four *Tiburones* appeared near the shipyard; they wanted revenge for the beating I gave them on our arrival day. They called to me: *"Musso, musso ven aqui, cobarde."* (*Mousse, mousse* come here, coward.) That did it, because I was not a coward.

I grabbed his thigh and bit him again. On the dock,
the four bad boys called the "Tiburones" were
enjoying the fight, clapping their hands.

Enraged, I quickly knocked out two of them,
so the other two ran away.

As soon as I got on the dock, all four of them jumped me. They were trying to hold me, so that one or two of them could beat the hell out of me; they instantly found out about my backup artilleries. I bit any parts of them that were within reach. In a hurry, they turned me loose. Then I began boxing and knocked down three of them. While they were on the ground, they hastily said, "*Musso, amigo, musso, amigo.*" (*Mousse* friend, *mousse* friend.) The fourth one, whom I discovered later was Julio, ran away while saying, "*Musso, enemiguito, musso, enemiguito.*" (*Mousse,* enemy, *mousse,* enemy.)

The three remaining *Tiburones*, Alberto, Juan, and Fabio, surrendered to me; I permitted them to come on board to wash the dishes, pots and pans, so they could eat the leftover food. The fourth, Julio, became frustrated because he could not come on board like the others and eat. So he prevented me from going ashore; whenever I went ashore he would bombard me with rocks. I would only hear his voice calling "*Musso, musso,*" but I never saw him. One day, he hit me with a large piece of brick that put a big knot on my head and caused it to bleed.

Furious, I reboarded the ship and kicked the other three *Tiburones* off the ship, just at lunchtime. I told them they could no longer eat on board unless they went and seized Julio for me immediately. Within a short time, they dragged Julio to me. I grabbed him by his shirt and gave him a good right hook that knocked him down. He got up and put himself in defensive position. He landed a couple of good punches on me; one punch caused bells to ring in my left ear, and the other gave me a black eye the following day. I gave him a few left and right hooks that knocked him down each time; then I hugged him and bit his back until he yelled, *"Musso, amiguito, musso, amiguito."* (Mousse, friend, Mousse, friend.) From then on, I became the leader of the *Tiburones*. The following day, Julio had a couple of black eyes, but all the *Tiburones* were on board cleaning and eating, and under my command, not Julio's.

On arrival day after my fight with the captain, everyone discovered that I was the owner's son. Since the captain had moved ashore, no one dared to ask me to do anything because they did not know just how much I could get away with. I no longer studied or worked; I had a real vacation. I only played and navigated in the river with the dinghy. We also rigged the dinghy with her lugsail. If there were no wind, the *Tiburones* would be the oarsmen; I would be at the rudder because I was the captain.

With the dinghy, we went upriver investigating until we reached two branches of the river. After a few trips upriver, we did anything that might provide us with additional thrills. We trailed baited fishing lines up and down the river. We located all the isolated places for our private beach parties. We made five slingshots, so our next cruise included fishing and hunting, as well as fruit picking while no one was looking. The first couple of cruises were very dull; fishing and fruit picking were too easy, but the hunting was very hard; the bushes were full of thorns. On the other cruises, people were happy to give us fruit, but we wanted to steal the fruit and have the owner chase us. The only fun was when Julio killed somebody's big red rooster. Julio cooked the rooster and made *"arroz con pollo,"* (chicken and rice) but there was not enough chicken for the amount of rice.

On the following trip upriver, we concentrated more on chicken hunting. When we located the chickens not far from the owner's house, they were friendly and came toward us, thinking that we were going to feed them. However, we wanted to feed on them. Juan bent down and picked up a big chicken, so we took off with it in Juan's arm. We sailed across the river to one of our secluded beaches. Lighting a driftwood fire, we prepared to skewer-cook our chicken and have a beach party. When the time came to kill the chicken, no one wanted to do it; we finally sailed back across the river and returned our friendly chicken to the place we had picked her up. Laughing and blaming each other for petting and getting too friendly with the chicken, we agreed that domesticated chicken hunting provides no thrills

Regardless of what happened on our chicken excursions, Julio decided to cook a real big pot of chicken and rice with lots of chicken in it. He said he knew where many chickens climbed a tree after 6:00 PM. Julio also said he knew how to make the chickens pass out and fall down from the tree. That evening, Julio arrived with a small pan with some crushed leaves in it. When he and I came to the tree with all the chickens on it, he lighted the mixture in the pan; smoke started to rise to the chickens, and they began falling down. Amazed, I busied myself picking up chickens and putting them in my bag. All of a sudden, a dog barked. Julio dropped the pan and dived between the barbed wire, saying, "*Musso, vamonos.*" (*Mousse*, let's go.)

With the dingy, trespassing and playing along the river's sides, I was the captain and leader of the "Tiburones."

Unlike Julio, I was not about to abandon my bag of chickens. Quickly, I swung the bag over the wire and dived under it. When I bent down to pick up the bag, a pair of strong hands grabbed me. The man released all the chickens and dragged me to the police station. He was the chickens' owner, and also the police station's sergeant; he locked me in a cell.

Julio ran to the ship and told the crew, "*Musso, en la carcel.*" (*Mousse* is in jail.) Julio knew the chickens belonged to the policeman, but I did not completely understand that part; even if I had understood, it would not have made any difference. The policeman saw Julio running, so he had Julio picked up and locked him in the cell next to mine while we waited for our parents.

When Captain Léopold arrived, the policeman greeted him and introduced himself as Sergeant Alsene. He explained to the captain that he had been keeping an eye on the *Tiburones* and me. Furthermore, he wanted to stop us from trespassing along the river banks using the dinghy, and playing pirate. Then he said, "Captain Léopold, with your cooperation, I want to stop those kids before they get into serious troubles."

"I am with you. What do you want of me?"

"You should forbid the *Tiburones* to board your ship and forbid your boy the use of the dinghy."

"Consider it done, Sergeant."

"Thank you, Captain, for your cooperation."

"What are you going to do with my boy?"

"I will release your boy without pressing charges against him or you, Captain."

"Thank you, Sergeant Alsene."

I was released to Captain Léopold. He ordered me to return on board, and said, "I will deal with you tomorrow."

"Thou shall not steal."

VOYAGE IX A
THE INTERPRETER

The following morning, Captain Léopold arrived early on board. The first thing he did was to arrange for the shipyard's foreman to remove the dinghy from the water and put it far away in the yard. Then he called the crew and told them the four boys called *Tiburones* were no longer allowed on board the ship. Also, I was restricted on board until further notice, and everyone was instructed to see that I did not leave the ship. The captain remained on board most of the day, taking care of various ship business. He also had me clean his cabin. Then the captain opened his curio locker. When he checked out his Scotch whiskey, he found three bottles were missing. Then he discovered one of his cigar boxes was half-empty.

Furious, Captain Léopold asked me, "What have you done with my cigars and whiskey?"

"Captain, I thought you would not object if I treated the custom officers and the *"carabiñeros"* (special police) who were on duty near the ship."

"You shall not give what does not belong to you."

"I believed the whiskey and the cigars were for treating shore officials, since you never used any of it yourself, except for that purpose."

"Let that be a lesson. You can give away only what belongs to you."

"Sorry, Sir, it will not happen again; I was only trying to be friendly with them."

"Since we arrived in Santo Domingo, you have been fighting and playing pirate on the river, yet you are not completely in control of your grammar. Here is the grammar book for you to study; put that time restricted on board to good use. I want you to know every spelling rule and all the various conjugation forms in that French grammar. Furthermore, you gave away my properties without my permission; therefore, you are no longer fit to share my cabin. Pack up your gear, get out of my cabin, and give me my keys. You will bunk in the cook's cabin with Hammed." With that, the captain left the ship.

The *Tiburones* were forbidden to come on board, and we lost our pirate ship, the dinghy. I was restricted on board the ship, but I had had the best vacation of my life and a good time while I was the *Tiburones'* leader.

Most of the crew felt sorry for me for getting into trouble with the police and the captain. The boatswain appeared to be the only one that enjoyed my misfortune and my punishment. He was happy to kick the *Tiburones* off the ship, and he said, "You bums and that vagabond *mousse* are through playing pirate on the river." The boatswain also found work for me to do; he wanted to keep me from my study, so I would get into trouble with the captain if I did not know the grammar.

At about 8:00 that morning, the captain arrived on board and waited for Williams, the interpreter. He had convinced the captain that he had a friend in the right place who could let him take some navigation equipment off the ship; however, Williams never showed up. I told the captain, "The guard and the officer at the gate drank your whiskey and smoked your cigars, so they are my friends. I could easily take the equipment off the ship."

"Are you sure?"

Nodding, I wrapped each item with dirty laundry and put them into two laundry bags. When the officers at the gate saw me with the laundry bags on my shoulders, they asked me, "*Mousso, donde va?*" (*Mousse*, where are you going?)

"*Me voy para el Chinito lavendero.*" (I am going to the Chinese laundry.)

"*Hasta luego.*" (See you later.)

"*Si senor, hasta luego.*" (Yes sir, see you later.)

I arrived at the "*mercado*," (marketplace) without any problems, and I waited for the captain. When he arrived, we waited for Williams because he might come here. Williams did not show up at the marketplace either, and the appointment time approached. Then the captain took a taxi to the meeting place and brought me along to carry the bags. When we arrived at the rendezvous, a man greeted us and introduced himself as Manuelo; he asked for Williams. The Captain told him Williams had not yet arrived. They agreed to wait for the interpreter. After a while they both became restless, and Manuelo began to speak in Spanish to the captain, but they did not understand each other. So I began to interpret for them, and they completed their negotiation and business successfully. The captain was surprised with my interpretation and amazed at my large Spanish vocabulary. He asked, "How did you learn Spanish so quickly?"

"Captain, I learned with the *Tiburones*, the Customs, and the Carabiñeros."

"Some good came out of your vagabond ways, then. So you got educated in Spanish by your friends?"

"Yes, Sir."

After we left Manuelo, the captain entered the first clothing store he saw and bought me an outfit exactly like the one he was wearing: a new white shirt, white shorts, white knee socks, and a new pair of brown shoes. He had me dress in the store, and tossed my old clothes in the wastebasket. True, my clothes were a bit shabby, but they were good enough to wear on board. Then the captain noticed the empty laundry bags that had contained the navigational equipment; he also tossed them into the wastebasket.

I said, "Thank you, Sir, for the new outfit." I thought the captain had rewarded me for the good interpretation I had done for him, but he had an additional plan.

When we left the clothing store, the captain said, "Let's go, I have another important appointment."

"With who?"

"I did not receive payment as scheduled for the freezer plant, and I must also pay the shipyard."

Dressed exactly like the captain, I carried the briefcase he had handed me, and we walked to the next meeting place. We entered a big building and went into a large office; first, we met the shipyard's manager, Émilio, and then a large elderly woman greeted us. She introduced herself as Senora Casanova and asked for Willams. The captain said, "No Willams," and he pointed at me and said, *"Mon fils, Georges."* (my son, Georges.)

"Oh, Captain, you have an impressive looking son."

"Thank you."

Then I started the interpretation for them. I was also able to read most of the contract because Spanish, like French, makes vocal sounds by a combination of alphabetical letters. I translated the best I could for the captain, although he appeared well acquainted with each subject. Senora Casanova acted as liaison for the purchaser of the freezer plant, the shipyard and Captain Léopold. Next, the captain acknowledged that the shipyard had fulfilled its contract and for the amount of money indicated. The shipyard's bill was deducted from the total price paid for the freezer plant, and at this time Captain Léopold received a certified check for the balance due him.

Captain Léopold and Émilio were both satisfied with the translation I did for them. After we left the office, the captain and Émilio returned to the clothing store. Captain Léopold bought me an additional two white outfits exactly like the first one, and Émilio, the shipyard's manager, bought me a beautiful all-leather suitcase. I could not find the right words to say thank you, so I smiled and just said, "Thanks." It certainly felt good to have done something right since our arrival in Santo Domingo two months ago. Then Captain Léopold said, "Well done, Joe-Joe; Émilio is returning to the yard; you go back with him. I have to meet Mademoiselle Colette from the French Embassy. Here is the key to my cabin; you have earned the right to move back in."

"Thank you, Sir."

Émilio drove back to the shipyard, and most of the crew saw my arrival near the gangway, all dressed up like the captain with my new suitcase. Hammed said, *"Ah, Mousse, tu as rencontré une Fée."* (Oh *mousse*, you met a Fairy Princess.)

"Ah, oui, Hammed." (Oh, yes, Hammed.)

I said nothing else to anyone; I just opened the owner's cabin, got in, and closed the door. Then I realized my restriction to the ship had lasted only a week; nevertheless, it is very hard to keep a good man—or a good boy—down.

In the morning, the captain arrived on board. He had to bring Hammed to the *"mercado,"* or (marketplace) to pick up immediate provisions. We also needed to place a special order for the ship's store to be delivered on sailing day, approximately a week from now, for the voyage to Saint Martin, by way of Puerto Plata, Dominican Republic. Captain Léopold wanted me to go with him to the marketplace; he had a free interpreter, and he intended to use him.

Oh Mousse, you met a fairy princess.

While there, he told Antonio, the manager, that I would be the one approving and signing for the provisions Hammed required. I also did the captain's bookkeeping for everything related to the ship. I went out with him sometimes during the evening, and when our outing ended too late, I slept on the settee in his hotel room office. In fact, I practically moved into the hotel; in the morning, I shined his brown shoes and mine, but he sent me back on board when Mademoiselle Colette visited.

On the fourteenth of July, Bastille Day, since not too many French people lived in Santo Domingo and *Putnick* was the only French ship in port, the French Ambassador invited the crew to a celebration. It was a real black tie gala; however, the crew could wear their Merchant Navy uniforms, if they preferred. Captain Léopold was surprised that the crew accepted the Ambassador's invitation and decided to buy black tie outfits if the captain would give them a draw. The crew said it was a rare opportunity to be invited to the French Embassy's gala, and they would not miss this occasion.

Captain Léopold agreed to give them money for the occasion, but he was busy negotiating for a load of cargo to Saint Martin. Therefore, he gave me the draw's logbook and the money for the crew. When I arrived on board, I explained why the captain could not be there, and that he had put me in charge. Furthermore, he had previously counted the money into separate envelopes and marked them with the crew member's name; additionally, the captain said, "Those who want the money, please sign the logbook and count the money immediately." Without any difficulties, the crew members signed the book and took their money. Then I told the boatswain, "Captain Léopold said to give the men sufficient time off to purchase their formal clothes."

Everything proceeded as scheduled; the men were happy with their new outfits. Antonio from the *mercado* had recommended a specialty store that took good care of them, and I went with them to interpret. Meanwhile, *Putnick* was made ready for sea and decorated for the 14th of July. Everyone waited impatiently for the celebration and our departure from Santo Domingo. With confidence, the crew expected Captain Léopold would, as customary, make the right decision for our destination.

The evening of July 14, in the captain's hotel room, I dressed in my new suit. The captain tied my first bow tie, and I surely appeared grown up wearing my first tuxedo. Then he sent me to the ship with instructions: "Tell the crew that the Ambassador's chauffeur will pick them up at 7 PM. Be ready on time." At 7 exactly, a mini-bus arrived; everyone was ready and well-dressed. After a half-hour drive, we arrived at a secluded resort mansion; Mademoiselle Colette greeted us and introduced the crew by announcing, "The crew of the famous sailing ship *Putnick*, from Nantes, France, owned and commanded by Captain Léopold." The French Ambassador himself greeted us and shook our hands; of course, I was the last one. The Ambassador asked, *"Qui est cet élégant jeune homme?"*

(Who is this elegant young man?)

"*Je suis le mousse, Monsieur L'Ambassadeur.*" (I am the deck boy, Mr. Ambassador.)

"*Ah! C'est toi! Je suis au courant de tes dons.*" (Oh, it is you! I heard about your talents.)

Various ambassadorial groups arrived, and each was properly announced. Then the orchestra played "*La Marseillaise,*" (the French National Anthem), followed by "*La Valse de L'Empereur,*" (The Emperor's Waltz). The French Ambassador and his wife opened the Grand Ballroom, and most couples followed with their partners and waltzed with dignity. For the first few dances, I only walked around the ballroom searching for a possible partner—there were many young girls, and most were either too young or too mature for me, but one attracted me as unique and lustrous. I approached her, speaking in Spanish, and she answered me in French: "*Mousse, merci de m'avoir inviter.*" (*Mousse*, thanks for inviting me.) "*Vous saviez que je suis le mousse. Je m'appelle Georges.*" (You knew I am the deck boy. My name is Georges.)

"*J' ai assister a votre presentation a L'Ambassadeur de France.*" (I heard your introduction to the French Ambassador.)

"*Je m'appelle Isabelle, je suis en vacance avec mes parents; nous sommes de Saint Martin.*" (My name is Isabelle, I am on vacation with my parents; we are from Saint Martin.)

We fit each other well and danced gracefully.

We danced together for most of the following dances. We stood out because we were the youngest couple on the floor. We fit each other well, and we danced so gracefully that, all of a sudden, we were in the middle of the floor, and everyone had stopped to watch us until the end of the waltz. Then Isabelle held my hand and guided me over to meet her parents. I first met her mother, and when we located her father, he was talking with Captain Léopold. Isabelle said, *"Papa, excuse moi, je voudrai te présenter mon ami Georges."* (Papa, excuse me, I would like to introduce my friend Georges.)

"Bonjour Georges, tu dances tres bien." (Hello, Georges, you are a good dancer.)

"Merci, Monsieur." (Thank you, Sir.)

"Captain Léopold, que fait ce jeune a bord?" (Captain Léopold, what is this young man doing on board?)

"Georges est l'apprenti; il est aussi mon fils." (Georges is the apprentice and also my son.)

"By chance, my Isabelle and your Georges found each other."

Both men laughed and continued their business conversation. Isabelle and I returned to the banquet, ate, drank, and danced together for the rest of the celebration. Then the crew returned to the ship.

In the early morning, Hammed and I went to the market with a list for sea store prepared by the captain. We could replace any item on the list, according to availability. I interpreted for Hammed, and finally we ordered sea store for the voyage from Santo Domingo to Puerto Plata. When we returned on board, the boatswain was missing; I informed the captain. The following day, our provisions arrived from the market and we loaded fuel and water. We were scheduled to sail with the inflow tide at 8:30 AM, the next day.

Captain Léopold had me clean his quarters because we would have three passengers occupying his cabin; a piano repairman arrived, who fixed and tuned the small piano. Later, a new entertainment center, radio and record player also arrived and were installed in the captain's cabin. Captain Léopold and I would occupy the cook's cabin, and Hammed would move into the foxhole, the crew's accommodation.

On the day of departure, at 8:00 AM, a limousine arrived at the gangway; to my surprise, Monsieur and Madame Guilloule and their daughter, Isabelle, came on board. I had not known that they were the passengers, and Monsieur Guilloule the charterer. Just before sailing, the French Consulate and the police informed Captain Léopold that the boatswain had been brutally beaten. He was in the hospital and would not be fit for duty for awhile. Monsieur Fernand, the boatswain, was known as a bad *hombre*, a nasty man when he had a drink too many; he would be repatriated by the French Consulate.

We sailed immediately for Puerto Plata; there, we would pick up a load of dry cargo for Le Marigot or Saint Martin. Since the boatswain missed the ship, Captain Léopold moved into the boatswain's cabin, and I moved back with Hammed. Monsieur Lambesc, a former sail maker, was promoted to boatswain, and he remained in the crew's quarters. Monsieur Lambesc also held a certificate of *patron* (person in charge of a coastal vessel).

So, we lost the battle of Santo Domingo because we left behind a man in the hospital and the *mousse* was in jail for two hours. However, we could have called this battle a draw. Since we lodged in this port for almost three months, our casualties could have been greater; besides, everyone was delighted that the boatswain missed the ship... especially me!

VOYAGE X
SAINT MARTIN, VIA PUERTO PLATA

After almost three months in Santo Domingo, we finally sailed from port. The freezer plant was sold and removed, the hull was properly repaired, and we had sold most of our fishing gear. *Putnick* was now a dry cargo ship, and we were on our way to Puerto Plata, Dominican Republic, to load our first dry cargo to be delivered at Le Marigot, Saint Martin.

The Guilloules were all three good sailors, and they wanted to participate in the sailing, the operation, and the ship's navigation watches. Therefore, Monsieur Guilloule spent most of his time in the 12-to-6 watches—the captain's watches. Madame Guilloule, Isabelle, and I were mainly in the 6-to-12 watches, Monsieur Lambesc's watches, but only during the day.

Our first day at sea was a beautiful one, and we navigated along the Dominican coast easily with a fair northeasterly wind. However, at sunset, Captain Léopold lowered and secured most of the sails for the night, except for one sail to reduce the ship's rolling. With the engine only, we continued for the rest of the night; the captain also adjusted our speed to arrive at Puerto Plata in the early morning.

During the first sea watch from departure, 9 a.m. to 12 noon, Isabelle steered the ship for a half-hour, and we took a few radar fixes off the coast. Then Monsieur Lambesc sent me to the galley to give Hammed a hand. Isabelle and her mother arrived in the galley and asked Hammed for permission to bake their favorite cake as dessert for supper; they spent most of the afternoon baking. During the evening watch after 6 PM, with Monsieur Lambesc's permission, I went to help the cook with the cleaning. Isabelle followed me and helped. When we returned on watch, Monsieur Lambesc helped us locate most of the constellations; then we found Polaris and checked our latitude using the North Star. The sea remained choppy with low swells, so we made good speed during the night. During the morning watch, we arrived in Puerto Plata, and were docked before 9 a.m.

The stevedores began loading the cargo immediately. The captain and the Guilloules went ashore to order fresh provisions for the voyage to Saint Martin. The captain returned alone and went to sleep, because he had been up most of the night along the Dominican coast. The stevedores loaded the cargo until 5 p.m. and knocked off until the next morning; we were scheduled to sail at 2 p.m. for Saint Martin. That evening before supper, everyone went to town except those on port watches. Therefore, we had a very short suppertime, so Hammed left most of the leftover food on the stove's warm plates, and other food in the refrigerator for the night lunch because later the crew would be hungry. Hammed completed his cleaning quickly and took off before me, for I had to finish washing the pots and pans. Then I went ashore with Pascal, our youngest *"matelot,"* (or first-class seaman).

After we passed the main street that contained most of the stores and the cinemas, we crossed the railroad track and arrived at a beautiful saloon, which had a bar on one side and an orchestra, including a singer, on the opposite. The orchestra was playing *"La Comparsita,"* a beautiful Argentine tango. Between the bar and the orchestra, a few couples were dancing. Among them, I saw Monsieur Lambesc; he was dancing with one of the hostesses. At the end of the tango, Monsieur Lambesc approached Pascal and me and said, "Pascal, what are you doing here with the *mousse?* You take him out of here immediately, and take him to one of the cinemas on the main street." Then he added, "Pascal, tomorrow I will talk with you."

I went to a good movie and watched a beautiful woman matador fighting a couple of mean bulls. At the intermission, I went to buy a *"gelado,"* (a frozen fruit-flavored refreshment on a stick). When I arrived at the stand's counter, I saw Isabelle and her parents; they were each licking a *gelado.* Madame Guilloule saw me first and called me, "Hey, *Mousse.*" When Isabelle saw me, she yelled, "Joe-Joe, Joe-Joe." She hugged me with a few swit kisses. Then she asked, "How do you like the movie?"

"I love it."

"Where are you seated?"

"In the front of the middle section."

"We are also seated in the middle section, but in the middle of it."

Madame Guilloule said, *"Assieds toi avec nous."* (You sit with us.)

We seated ourselves quickly before the movie resumed. At the end of the movie, Monsieur Guilloule asked, "How about a snack before returning on board?" We answered simultaneously, *"Oh, oui."* (Oh, yes.) Then we entered a large café that had inside and outside tables. We asked the host to seat us outside because we wanted to watch the promenade and the walkers as we enjoyed a plate of delicious *"paella"* (chicken, sausage, pork, shrimp, mussel, and yellow rice cooked together). We spent more than an hour seated at our outside table eating, sipping our soft drinks, criticizing, and laughing at the people as they passed by us. We also saw some of our crew pass on the promenade, but they did not see us; they were too busy talking and holding hands with their new friends. Finally, we got tired of watching the promenade. We returned to the ship and went to bed.

At 8 a.m. the next morning, the stevedores returned and resumed the loading. Meanwhile, we took on fresh provisions, fuel, and water. Madame Guilloule added to our provisions all of her family's favorite foods, and told Hammed she would spend some time in the galley with him. The loading of cargo was completed at 3 p.m., and we sailed immediately for Le Marigot, Saint Martin. The passengers had a good time; I knew because I was with them. The crew also had a good time. They were bragging about their conquests and the fun they had had. They said it had been a good port, and we won the battle of Puerto Plata.

By five that evening, most of the sails were up, and we knocked off for supper, except for those who were on sea watch. I was on watch until midnight, but Monsieur Lambesc usually sent me to help the cook. I had three duties: galley boy, deck boy, and deck cadet. During my sea watches, I learned how to sail, practiced navigation, and worked in the galley whenever possible.

On this particular voyage during the day, Isabelle and her mother shared most of my duties; they also participated in the captain's watch. The Guilloules handled the sails, navigated, steered the ship, and cooked. Since departure, we sailed on a northeast course on the starboard tack; this course would keep us to the north and well clear of Puerto Rico. We wanted to go east, up the wind, and sometimes we had to steer northeast in one tack and southeast in the other tack to compensate and to keep the vessel progressing on the desired east direction. It is most important to keep the vessel's course, well clear of any obstruction or nearby island.

After 3 a.m. we were on a northeast course—just before,

we had crossed the traffic to and from Mona Pass (between Espaniola and Puerto Rico). The quartermaster, Boudin, changed the ship's course without the captain's order. Monsieur Guilloule, who was in the captain's watch, noticed the course change and called the captain.

Using violent words, Boudin accused the captain of directing the ship toward a rendezvous with one of the German submarines that patrolled this area. He also called Captain Léopold 'De Saxe,' a German from Alsace who wanted to supply his compatriots with provisions from our ship's cargo. Furthermore, Boudin said Saint Martin was not to the northeast, as the ship was heading since our departure; the course should have been southeast and toward Saint Martin. He also accused Monsieur Guilloule of being the principal German liaison engaged in supplying provisions to the Germans from the cargo which belonged to Monsieur Guilloule, a German himself.

Captain Léopold called the emergency crew, and Boudin was brought into custody and thrown into the ship's brig because of his violence. This crew member had committed a serious infraction that could have resulted in a shipwreck with possible loss of many lives. On arrival in Saint Martin, Boudin would be turned over to the French marine administrator for disciplinary action. Captain Léopold could not allow the man freedom to resume his sabotage.

With the quartermaster in the ship's brig for the rest of

the voyage, the crew was short one man. Monsieur Guilloule, who possessed a deck officer certificate, replaced Boudin and signed on the ship's article as *"matelot"* (able seaman).

The disturbance caused by Boudin's accusation and his being taken into custody brought all hands on deck, so our first full day at sea commenced early and was a long one. In the morning, Isabelle and her mother spent most of their time cooking with Hammed; at dinner and suppertime, we ate rare dishes and had fancy desserts. They used every dish, pot, and pan in the galley, which caused additional washing for me, but it was worth it. Besides, Isabelle always helped me with the galley's cleaning.

In the afternoon, the wind backed around and changed its direction from southeast to northeast. We came about to the port tack and sailed at ease on Boudin's desired course—southeast— but the course was now well clear of any obstruction. We were heading for a position north of the Virgin Islands; after landfall, we would set out for Saint Martin.

In the afternoon, Isabelle and her mother practiced handling the sails and steering the ship. Everyone enjoyed having the Guiloules on board; life on the ship was more like a home with soft music in the background throughout the ship. Because they were so busy, they did not play the piano, which Captain Léopold had repaired for them, so we had to ask Isabelle to play for us.

The evening before arrival, after supper, the Guilloules agreed to play for the crew. Isabelle sang and played the piano, her mother played the flute, Monsieur Guilloule played his violin, and they switched instruments at the end of each song. It was a beautiful concert: on the open deck, under a full moon, with a sky full of stars. Every one of the crew attended and enjoyed the music—except Boudin, who remained in the ship's brig. He might have heard the music, but he missed the sight of the beautiful scenery.

Captain Léopold adjusted our speed to make landfall in the morning and to navigate through the islands during daylight. We made good speed and arrived in Saint Martin at 6:30 p.m. During the night, we remained at the anchorage, and the next morning the stevedores commenced the discharge of our cargo into barges. The Guilloules said goodbye to the crew and thanked them for making them feel at home while on board. Isabelle and her mother could not hold back their tears at the end of their goodbyes. Then Captain Léopold went ashore with them.

When the captain returned, he told me Monsieur Guilloule would pick us up at 4 p.m. I dressed casually, and was ready on time. We first visited the Guilloules' salt-producing business, and after that they invited us for the evening meal. On our arrival, Madame Guilloule, her parents, and Isabelle welcomed us into their home, a beautiful French colonial house decorated with

Marigot St. Martin — St. Maarten harbor.

designer marble, chandeliers, and a gorgeous staircase. After
the traditional French *aperitif*, we had a fancy supper followed
by a delicious homemade coconut ice cream. Next, Isabelle and
her friends played their music, and the youngsters danced for
a while. Of course most of Isabelle's dances were reserved for
me, then just before the party ended we escaped into the back

porch where we hugged and kissed. Obviously, her parents had organized the evening for Isabelle as a welcome home party.

The evening ended with a joyful goodbye, this time without tears. Monsieur Guilloule drove the captain and me to the ship. We were surprised to find most of the crew on board. They had been ashore, but only for a short time. The three-months port time in Santo Domingo had left them broke, and they were saving their money for the next port. The old sailor's tall tale would have gone: "The battle of Saint Martin was postponed because of battle fatigue." We were scheduled to sail the next day after supper for Fort de France, Martinique.

The Guilloule's home — a beautiful French Colonial

VOYAGE X1
FORT-DE-FRANCE

In Saint Martin, we loaded fresh provisions, fuel, and fresh water. The stevedore also loaded *Putnick* with rock salt from Monsieur Guilloule's warehouse for a consignee in Fort-de-France. Just before sailing, Monsieur Guilloule came on board with his sea bag and suitcase and said, "I am still a member of the crew, and I am not about to miss the ship." Monsieur Guilloule was also the charterer; he bunked in the owner's cabin with Captain Léopold. After supper, most of the sails were already up, so we picked up anchor and got underway for Fort-de-France, Martinique.

At sea the next day, I felt sick, and I was shivering with a fever. Captain Léopold gave me some aspirin and sent me to bed. After a swift and smooth voyage, we arrived in Fort-de-France. On arrival, the health official removed me from the ship and took me to the hospital, because I had what appeared to be yellow fever, which I probably had contracted in the Ozama River of Santo Domingo. In the afternoon of the following day, Captain Léopold arrived at the hospital with Papa Maurice, my biological father, and Maman Camille, my step-mother; he owned a plantation and lived in Martinique. Although I was sick, we were happy to see each other after ten years of separation, thanks to World War II.

During my two weeks' stay in *L'hôpital Colonial*, a military hospital, Papa Maurice and Maman Camille visited me often. They brought me games, homemade cakes, fruits, candies, and writing paper, which I used to write to Isabelle. Hammed, Monsieur Lambesc, Pascal, and most of the crew visited me too. When Captain Léopold and Monsieur Guilloule visited, they informed me of Monsieur Guilloule's desire to purchase *Putnick*; he liked the ship because of her design, accommodations, carrying capacity, and economical operation. Monsieur Guilloule wanted the ship for his own pleasure, and at the same time he would haul out, or carry, his rock salt and other cargo throughout the islands. Before my release from the hospital, Monsieur Guilloule and his partner had completed the purchase of the ship.

Most of the crew agreed to stay with Monsieur Guilloule and Captain Gautier, his partner. Three men from *"Terre-Neuve"* (Newfoundland) would be repatriated. Most important, Captain Léopold wanted to return to France to search for his family, displaced after World War II. Now Monsieur Guilloule wanted me to stay with him—not as the *mousse*, deck boy, or galley boy, but as deck cadet with a good salary. My only duty would be to assist Captain Gautier, practice navigation and seamanship until I graduated to serve as a deck officer. This was a very good opportunity, with a good future for me. Of course, I was tempted; in addition, I would see Isabelle often. But accepting this offer would mean abandoning Captain Léopold, who was so important to me. Therefore, I decided to return to France with Captain Léopold.

After a swift and smooth voyage, we arrived in Fort-de-France, Martinique.

The day of my release from the hospital, Monsieur Guilloule and Captain Gautier were taking over the ship. Captain Léopold and I were removed from the ship's article, and afterward Captain Léopold handed me an envelope and said, "Joe-Joe, here is your share for all the good work you have done. I have been saving it for you."

"Thank you, Captain. I thought I was not entitled to any share."

"Legally, you are not, but you have earned it the hard way. You worked for it."

The envelope contained a check of 25,000 francs— approximately $5,000. That same day, Captain Léopold took me to a bank and opened an account in my name, in care of Captain Léopold or Papa Maurice. That was a lot of money in 1945, especially since in addition to my feeding, lodging, and upkeeping, I also received an education.

The next day, Papa Maurice and Maman Camille invited Captain Léopold, Monsieur Guilloule, and Captain Gautier for Sunday dinner at their plantation home. They butchered a lamb for the occasion and also invited my father's sister *"Tante"* (Aunt) Carmaine with her husband *"Tonton"* (Uncle) François. After a few *"aperitifs"* and *"amuse-gueules"* (cocktail snacks), everyone got chummy. The dinner table was set with the name of each person marked, but the guests sat near their drinking or talking partners, ignoring the obvious reserved seats. Then the dinner got started, but the eating, the drinking, and talking continued until the end, everyone laughing happily.

Uncle François was the assistant director of the French Lines, a shipping company established in Martinique. He offered Captain Léopold a position as *Second Capitaine*, Chief Officer, on board one of the company's ships, which was returning to

France.

I objected and said, "Uncle François, what about me? I arrived with Captain Léopold, and I should leave with him." Then I added, "Uncle, if you cannot find me any job on board that ship, I want to go as a passenger."

Captain Léopold said, "Jo-Joe, it would be best that you get your license first. Then you could rejoin me as an apprentice pilot in Saint Nazaire, but you must have a license."

Captain Léopold also explained that he would prepare the necessary papers, and with my sea time, I would be allowed to sit for the examination without further training. Since the exam was scheduled for the end of the year, he would enroll me in the Nautical School, where I would learn how to successfully pass the examination. Papa Maurice, Monsieur Guilloule, and Captain Gautier agreed with Captain Léopold's planning for me. It became a *done deed*, and leaving with Captain Léopold was not one of my options—nor was staying with Monsieur Guilloule and Captain Gautier.

The following week, Captain Léopold sailed to France on board the *Aquarius*, a passenger and cargo combination vessel. About a week later, the *Aquarius* approached the coast of France where she hit a mine, blew up, and sank. Most of the crew and passengers survived, but unfortunately, Captain Léopold was among the missing. This bad news distressed me; I became disoriented, and I wanted to cry, but I remembered one of

Captain Léopold's orders four years ago when I was crying for my mother: "Stop that sissy, silly crying immediately. What kind of seaman are you?" Then he had shouted: *"I want you to be 'A brave mousse, a brave mousse', and that is a permanent order."*

Now I realized how lucky we were when Captain Léopold first met with a mine caught in our fishing net. Because of the captain's careful handling, the mine did not explode, and the experts in Dunkerque defused it. Four years earlier, at the beginning of our fishing voyage, a mine had threatened our lives and Captain Léopold had saved his ship and his crew. Now, at the end of this long voyage, with the captain nearly home, yet another mine beyond his control took his life.

I managed to stay in the Nautical School until the summer vacation. All my family and friends tried to console me in my grief for Captain Léopold. Uncle François suggested a short trip during the summer vacation would help me cope with my grief. So, he sent me as a crew member on the recently purchased French Lines ship the *Morbihan*, which was sailing from Mobile, Alabama, to Fort-de-France. Three weeks later, the ship arrived in Fort-de-France without me; I had deserted in Mobile. Then I sailed as a crewmember on board Panamanian, Norwegian, Swedish, and American flag ships. I felt destiny had cheated me out of my greatest mentor. So, trying to bury my grief, I went wild. Uncontrolled, I started to visit bars and nightclubs throughout the world, disregarding all the good

177

habits I had learned with Captain Léopold. Soon I began to get into trouble with emigration officials in various ports because I did not have a valid passport with the proper visa. All of the French Consulates which I visited refused to issue me a passport, because they quickly found out I was a deserter.

On board the *Aquarius*, Captain Léopold returned to France.

I returned to Fort-de-France four years later for a visit, and at the same time to get a new passport to resume my seagoing adventures. To my surprise, I was arrested and court-martialed as a deserter. Of course, my family got me off the hook without the jail time that usually came along with the charges; however, my seaman document was voided. I had even forgotten about all the French money that Captain Léopold had deposited in the bank for me. Untouched for four consecutive years, the money had grown considerably.

With this French money and the money I had saved during four years on board tramp ships, I thought I was rich. Since I had never forgotten the beautiful black motorcycle Monsieur Carméné used to give me a ride on when I was a kid, I searched, found, and bought a motorcycle exactly like the one Monsieur Carméné owned. With my motorcycle, I had a hell of a good vacation in Martinique. Even though I was the leader of the *Tiburones* for three months in Santo Domingo, this time remained unequivocally the best vacation of my life.

With the help of my family in Martinique, I finally obtained a new French passport with the proper visa and returned to New York. I was already a member of the National Maritime Union, so I got jobs from the union on board United States flagships as able seaman and boatswain, until I became a United States citizen. Thereafter, I promptly sat for the examination for Third Officer, Second Officer, and Chief

Officer, and finally became licensed to serve as Master of United States Steam or Motor Vessels of any Gross Tons upon Oceans. Thanks to Captain Léopold's teachings, I successfully and easily passed all of the United States Coast Guard License Officer Examinations. It appeared that Captain Léopold had passed on to me most of his wits, aptitude and skills. I will always remember Captain Léopold as the real Master, who is living within me, and I will always follow his rules and recommendations for the rest of my life.

Ten years after I first left Saint Nazaire, I returned and searched for my friends, family and Captain Léopold's family. I did not find my mother or any of my best friends, who included Monsieur Carméné, Monsieur Bernard, and Madame Léopold; they were all dead and buried during World War II. I found only Captain Léopold's daughter, Hildelite, who was now married, living with her husband and children. Hildelite cried, saying, "Joe-Joe, Joe-Joe, you are alive; I thought you had died with my father." She welcomed me as if I were a lost brother, and her children called me *"Tonton"* (Uncle) Joe-Joe. I was the only person close to her father just a week before his death; she wanted to talk only about the long voyage which I had made with her father. I also wanted to talk about my mother and her mother, Madame Léopold, since we were neighbors. Hildelite told me that both of our mothers and her brother had died instantly during a bombardment.

Hildelite and I returned to the shipyard dock where Captain Léopold and I had hugged and kissed Madame Léopold and my mother goodbye at the beginning of the voyage. That trip was a four-week fishing trip, but it lasted more than four years. At that time, we did not know we were saying our last goodbyes to our beloved Madame Léopold and my mother. I will always remember the day Captain Léopold and I left, and the motorboat that took us to the ship. I could see my mother and Madame Léopold waving with their handkerchiefs. When we were on board and sailed away, I continued waving to them until they faded away in the distance. But they will always remain in my memory as I last saw them.

I could see my mother and Madame Léopold waving
with their handkerchiefs; I continued waving
goodbye to them until they faded away.

SAILOR'S TERMINOLOGY

ALL HANDS: the complete deck's crew or the complete ship's crew
AFT: toward the stern
ABAFT: aft of, or behind
ABEAM: directly off the vessel's side
AMIDSHIPS: the middle of the vessel
ASTERN: going backward, toward the stern
ABACK: sails are pressed against the mast
ALOFT: above the deck
ANCHOR'S AWEIGH: anchor has cleared the bottom
BACK AROUND: the wind changes direction to the left
BEAM SEA: waves run at right angle to the ship's side
BAFFLING: confusing
BEAR A HAND: assist, help
BELAY: make fast
BERTH: sailor's bed; a vessel's place in port
BIGHT: loop of a rope or a wire
BILGE: a vessel's bottom
BLOCK: metal or wood shell holding pulley wheels
BINNACKLE: housing for the ship's compass

BOATSWAIN: a first class seaman in charge of the deck crew
BOSUN: short for boatswain
BOARDED: went aboard
BOLLARD: heavy post used to secure ropes
BOOM: a spar on a fore-and-aft line
BOW: front end of a vessel
BOWLINE: rope to hold the forward end; a knot forming a loop
BOWSPRIT: spar projecting beyond the bow
BOW WASH: waves made by the ship's forward motion
BRACE: controlling horizontal motion
BREACH: to break the water's surface
BROACH TO: accidentally swing sideways to the wind or the waves
BULKHEADS: inboard walls of a ship
BULWARKS: railing along a vessel's side
BUNTLINES: ropes to furl a square sail
BY THE MARK: lead line marked at 2, 3, 4 and upward by fathoms
BY THE DEEP—FIVE: depth 5 fathoms (30 ft)

CABLE: chain or rope attached to the anchor

CANTED OVER: heeled or laying toward one side

CAPSTAN: vertical drum-like cylinder for pulling on a rope

CUTWATER: lower edge of ship's stem

CREW: personnel to operate a ship

COXSWAIN: helmsman in command of a boat

CHAIN PLATES: flat bars attached to the hull's sides holding the lower ends of the shrouds

CLEW: lower corners on a square sail

COURSES: the lowest square sails

CRINGLE: a loop woven into the border of a sail

CHRONOMETERS: accurate clocks used for navigation

CRACK HER: set all possible sails

CUMSHAW: a present to welcome ashore in the Oriental countries

COMPASS POINT: direction marked on a compass

DOCKERS: workers on the docks or piers

DINGHY: a small rowboat

DECK: ship's floor

DECKHOUSES: enclosed structures on the deck

DAVIT FALLS: wires or ropes for lowering or raising a boat

DOWNHAULS: ropes for pulling down sails

DAVY JONES' LOCKERS: the bottom of oceans; the keeper of sailors' souls

EASE HER UP: head her toward the wind to reduce stress; or reduce the helm to slow her speed of swinging while turning

EIGHT BELLS: time to change any one of the three sea-watches, a.m. & p.m., 4, 8, and 12

FLUKE: The flattened end of an anchor arm which bites into the ground

FOREPEAK: storage space in the lower part of the bow

FORECASTLE: a superstructure at the bow

FORE: toward the bow

FORE-AND-AFT: bow and stern

FOREMAST: forward mast

FORESAIL: foremast's lowest sail

FORE TOPMAST STAYSAIL: a triangular sail

FURL: roll and secure sails

FRAP: tightly bind with ropes

FRESHENING: winds increasing

FULL AND BY: sailing close to the wind

FULL FOR STAYS: before tacking, steer away from the wind for good speed

FREEING PORT: opening for water to run overboard

GRAPNEL: small anchor with four hooked arms, fluke-like

GUNWALE: upper edge of a small boat's side

GRATING: latticework platforms

GRASSED: scraped

GEAR: a vessel's equipment

GATES: doors at entrance of locks

GANTLINE: temporary use of rope

GALLEY: the kitchen in a ship

GAFF: spar holding the top of fore-and-aft sail

GALE: 35 to 56 mph winds

HELM: the tiller or steering wheel

HELMSMAN: the man steering the ship

HARD OVER: bring rudder all the way to either side

HAULED HOME: completely pulled into place

HEAVING THE LEAD: with a lead line, finding the depth of water

HEAVER: a steel spike with a wood handle

HEAVING LINE: a small rope weighted at one end

HALYARD: tackle for raising gaffs and sails

HEAD: top edge of a sail, or the front of a vessel

HEADSAIL: triangular sail at the front of a vessel

HOWSEPIPE: holes in the bow for the anchor chain

HAWSER: large rope for towing or tying up a vessel

HATCHWAY: an opening in the deck

HOLLY STONE: to clean wood decks with sandstone

HOOVE CLEAR: pull free

HOOVE TO: vessel lying head to the wind

JUNKS: small Chinese vessel

JURY RIG: for temporary use

JIB: triangular headsail

JIBBOM: spar extending beyond the bowsprit

KNOTS: speed of a vessel in nautical miles per hour; or interlace to join two ropes

KETCH: a two-mast sailing vessel with the shorter mast aft

KEEL: the backbone of a vessel's structure

KITES: the light sails of a vessel

KNOCK OFF: stop work
LASHING ROPE: rope for tying down or securing things
LANDFALL: land's first sighting
LAND HO: lookout's yell upon first seeing land
LADDER: any vertical stair in a ship
LAUNCH: to put a boat or a vessel into the water
LAZARETTE: storeroom in the stern
LUFF HER UP: turn the vessel bow into the wind
LUBBER LINE: a line on the forward side of the compass representing the bow of the vessel
LOWER TOPSAILS: square sails directly above the course
LEECH: side edge of a square sail
LEE: the side away from the wind
LEEWARD: toward the lee side
LIST: lean to one side
LIGHTERS: barges to carry cargo
LIBERTY: permission to go ashore
MAIN DECK: the principal deck
MASTHEAD: upper end of the mast, above the crosstrees

MAINMAST: the principal or tallest mast
MAIN SHROUDS: the rigging supporting the mainmast
MAIN YARD: the lowest yard on the mainmast
MAIN COURSE OR MAIN: lowest sail on the mainmast
MIZZENMAST: the third mast of a three-mast vessel
MIZZEN-SHROUDS: the rigging supporting the mizzenmast
MAKE FAST: secure, belay
MAKE SAIL: unfurl, set the sails
MAUL: a heavy hammer
MARLINE: tarred, two-strand hemp cord
MARLINGSPIKE: tapered iron spike used for wire splicing
MASTER: the commander of a merchant ship
MATE: one of a vessel's deck officers
MOOR: to anchor, to secure to a pier
MEET HER: to counteract the vessel's swing with the rudder
MUSTER: a legal assembly of the crew
NAUTILUS SHELL: a pearly spiral seashell
NAIAD: water nymph
OILSKINS: wet weather garments

OLD SALTS: elderly seamen
OLD MAN: the captain's nickname
PORT: left side of a vessel when facing forward
PALM: sailor's thimble for sewing
PRICKERS: pointed tools used for canvas work
POOP: the enclosed space of the main deck at the stern
POOP RAIL: rail around the poop deck
PROW: the bow, the front of a vessel
POINTS: one point of the compass is 11 ¼ degrees
PITCH: rock fore and aft
PIPE: a series of notes blown on the bosun's whistle call
PIPE THE WATCH BELOW: to relieve the watch on deck
PINTLES: pivot pins on which a rudder hangs
PIER HEAD: the outer end of a pier
PAYED OFF: turned away from the wind
PAINTER: rope at the bow of a small boat
QUARTER: sides of a vessel near the stern
QUARTERDECK: after part of the main deck
RUNNING FREE: sailing before the wind

RUNNING GEAR: the moving rigging
RINGTAIL: light-weather sail extending the spanker
RINGBOLT: an eyebolt with a ring
RIGGING: all the ropes and gear
RIGGERS: workers who install rigging
ROYALS: sails above the topgallants
ROPE YARN: one thread of a strand of rope
RHUMB LINE: constant course
ROUSE: wake up, get up
REEF POINT: foreshorten a sail
RED LEAD: rust-resistant paint
SHEET: rope controlling the clew of a sail
SHEAVE: wheel of a block
SHEATING: planking on the inboard
SETTEE: a long seat
SCUPPERS: deck drains along the deck's side
SCUDDING: running before a gale with reduced or no sail
SCOW: flat-bottomed barge
SCHOONER: a vessel with fore-and-aft sails
SCUTTLE: deliberately sink a ship

SALVING: saving from destruction

SHIP WATER: to have seas wash on board

STEM: upright timber at the from end of the hull

STEMSON: inner structure of the stem

STERN: after end of the hull

STERN POST: upright timber at the after end of the hull

STANCHION: upright post

STARBOARD: right side of a vessel when facing forward

STAYS: fore-and-aft standing rigging

STAYSAILS: triangular fore-and-aft sails

STAND BY FOR STAY: order, prepare to tack a vessel

SQUARE-RIGGED: having square sails on yards set across the masts

SQUARE IN THE YARDS: brace the yard 90 degrees across the keel

SQUALLY: raining with violent gusts of wind

SPAR: mast, gaff, yard, and boom

SPOKES: radial spindles on a steering wheel

SPYGLASS: a telescope

SPINDRIFT: loose spray flying over the sea

SOUTHWESTER: a waterproof hat

SOUNDING LINE: a line marked with a lead on one end for measuring depths in fathoms

SKYSAIL YARDS: yards above the royal yards

SKYSAILS: sails above the royal

SHORES: temporary supports

STEADY AS SHE GOES: hold the vessel's head as ordered

SHROUDS: fixed rigging supporting the mast

STERNSON KNEE: part of the stern post

STUDDINGSAILS: light sails extending beyond square sails

STOW: put away or store

STOVE: holed or broken

SIGNAL FLAGS: flags for transmitting messages

SIGN ON: put your name on the ship's articles for the voyage

TRADE WINDS: winds from NE and SE between 30 N and 30 degrees S latitudes

TURNING TOP: capsizing

TACK: change course by turning ship's head into the wind

TACKS: ropes from lower corners of courses

TACKS AND SHEETS: order, to haul up clews of main course and crossjack preparatory to mains' haul

TACKLE: two blocks and a rope arrangement

TARPAULINE: heavy, water-repellent canvas

THIMBLE: circular fitting around which rope is spliced to form an eye

TILLER: a bar on the rudderhead; to turn rudder

THWART STRINGERS: wood strips inside of boat to hold the thwarts

THWART: crosswise seats in a boat

TOPGALLANT: above the topmast

TOPSAIL: the sail above a course

UNDER WAY: when a vessel is moving

VESSEL: a construction that floats

VANG: a rope to control the gaff

VEER: the wind change direction to the right

WEATHER SIDE: toward the windward side

WEATHER LEECH: windward leech of a square sail

WINDLASS: used to haul in the anchor chain

WINDJAMMER: any sailing vessel

WINDWARD: direction from which the wind is blowing

WHEELHOUSE: a house for the steering station

WAKE: turbulent water stern of a moving ship

WATCH: 4 to 8 to 12 to 4; the crew's duty period

YARN: to tell a sea story

YOKE LINES: ropes used to steer a boat

YAWL: a 2-masted sail boat with the shorter mast aft of rudder

YARD: horizontal spar crosswise on the mast

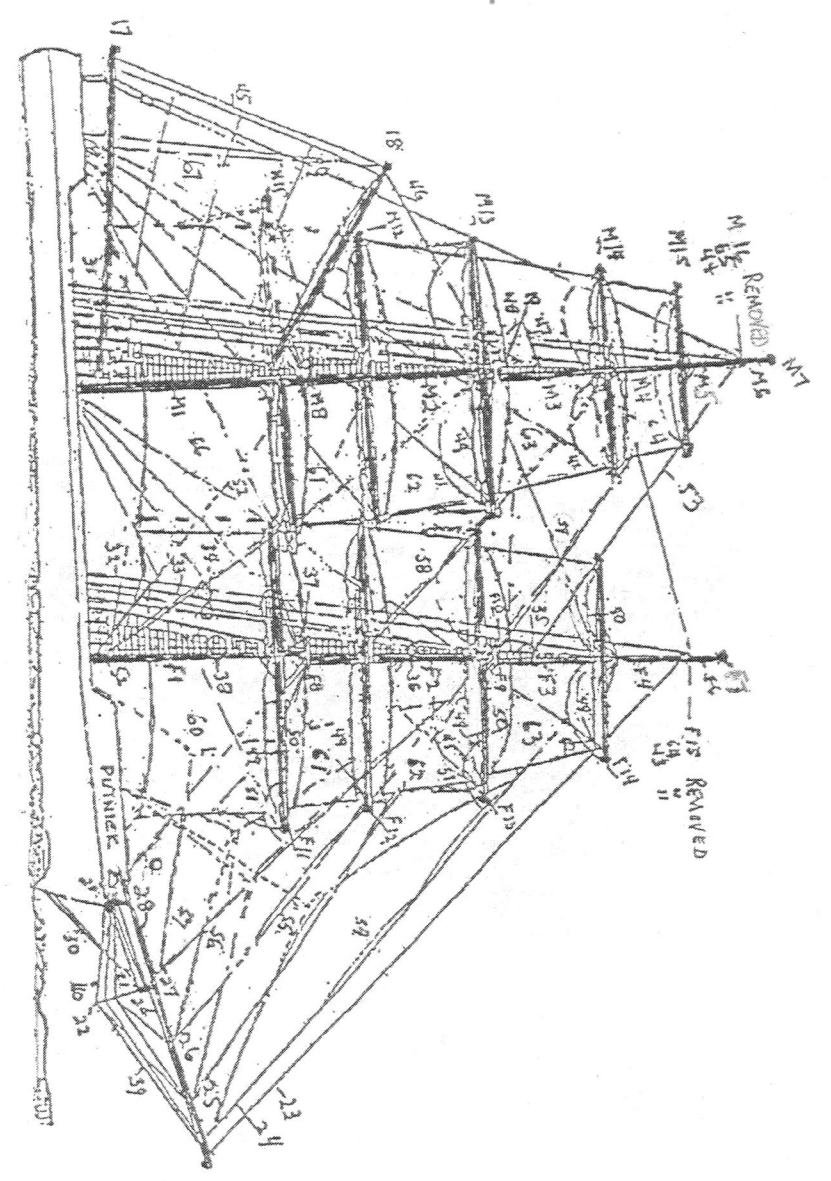

NOMENCLATURE

SPARS

F: foremast, M: mainmast;
Yards take the name of their
mast.

1. Lowermast
2. Topmast
3. Topgallant mast
4. Royalmast
5. Skysail mast
6. Pole
7. Truck
8. Top
9. Topmast crosstrees
10. Backstay spreaders
11. Lower yard
12. Lower topsail yard
13. Upper topsail yard
14. Topgallant yard
15. Royal yard
16. Skysail yard
17. Spanker boom
18. Spanker gaff
19. Signal gaff
20. Jib boom
21. Bowsprit
22. Martingale boom or
    dolphin striker

STANDING RIGGING

Stays take the name of the mast
they are on.

23. Royal stay
24. Topgallant stay or flying
    jib stay
25. Outer jib stay
26. Inner jib stay
27. Topmast stay
28. Jib boom guys
29. Bowsprit shrouds
30. Inner and outer bobstays
31. Skysail mast backstays
32. Royal backstays
33. Topgallant backstays
34. Topmast backstays
35. Topgallant shrouds
36. Topmast shrouds
37. Futtock shroud
38. Lower shrouds
39. Inner and outer martingale
    stays
40. Back ropes
41. Upper topsail lift
42. Topgallant lift
43. Royal lift (removed from
    foremast)
44. Skysail lift (removed)
45. Spanker boom lift
46. Spanker gaff span

47. Signal gaff lift
48. Signal gaff vangs
49. Footrope
50. Stirrup
51. Flemish horse
52. Main stay
53. Skysail mast stay
0. Fore stay

SAILS

Sails take the name of the mast they are flying on. Staysails take the name of the stay they are flying on.

54. Flying jib or fore topgallant staysail

55. Outer jib staysail
56. Inner jib staysail
57. Topmast staysail
58. Topgallant staysail
59. Royal staysail
60. Fore course or foresail
61. Lower topsail
62. Upper topsail
63. Topgallant sail
64. Royal sail (removed from foremast)
65. Skysail (removed from mainmast)
66. Main course or mainsail
67. Spanker

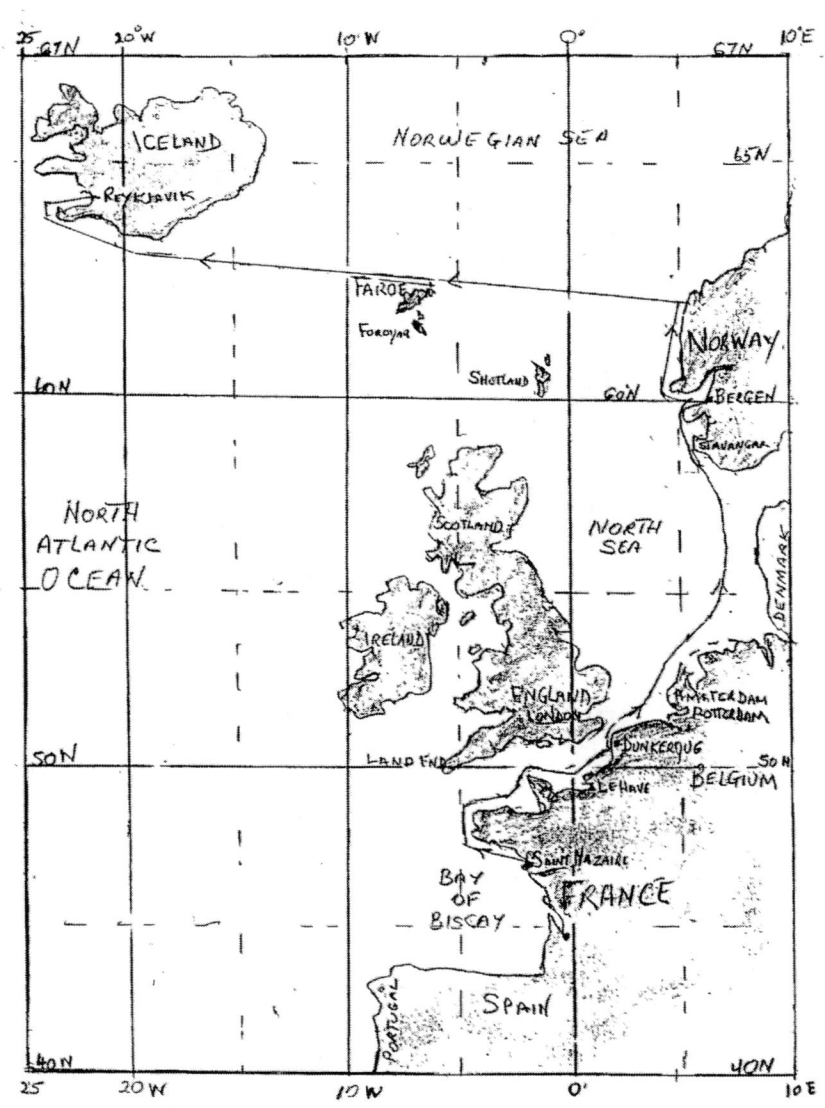

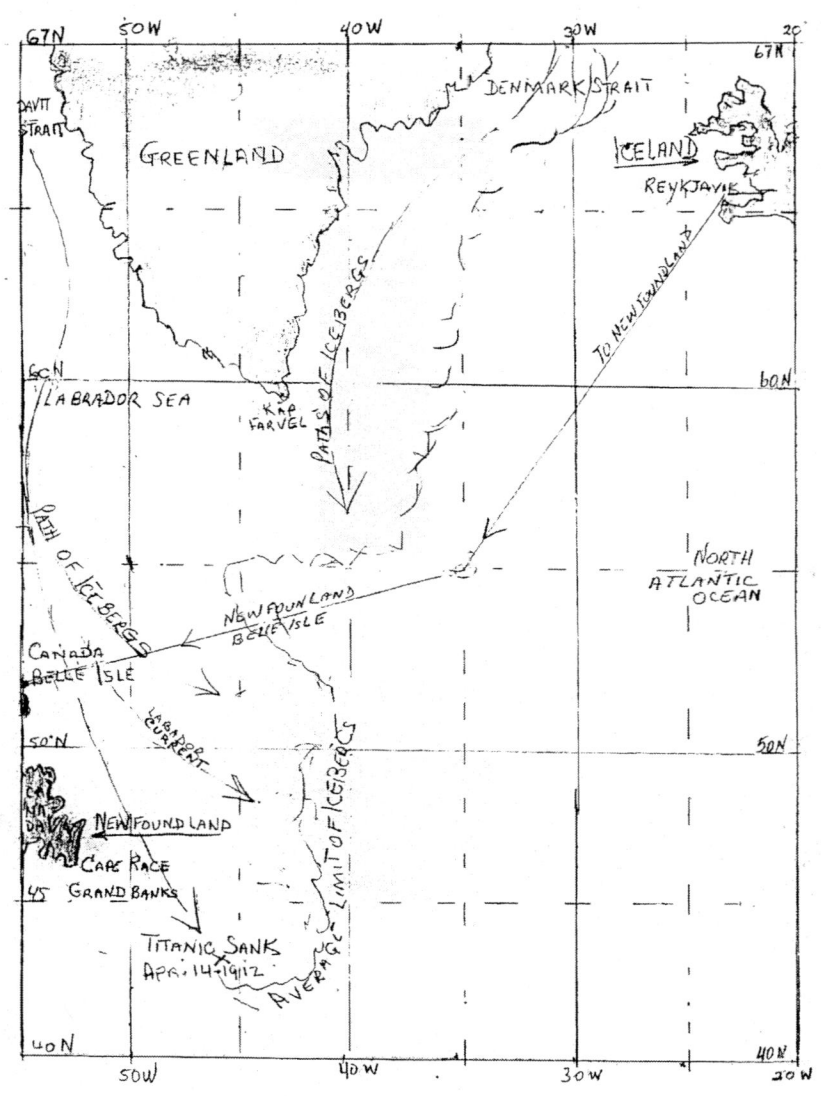

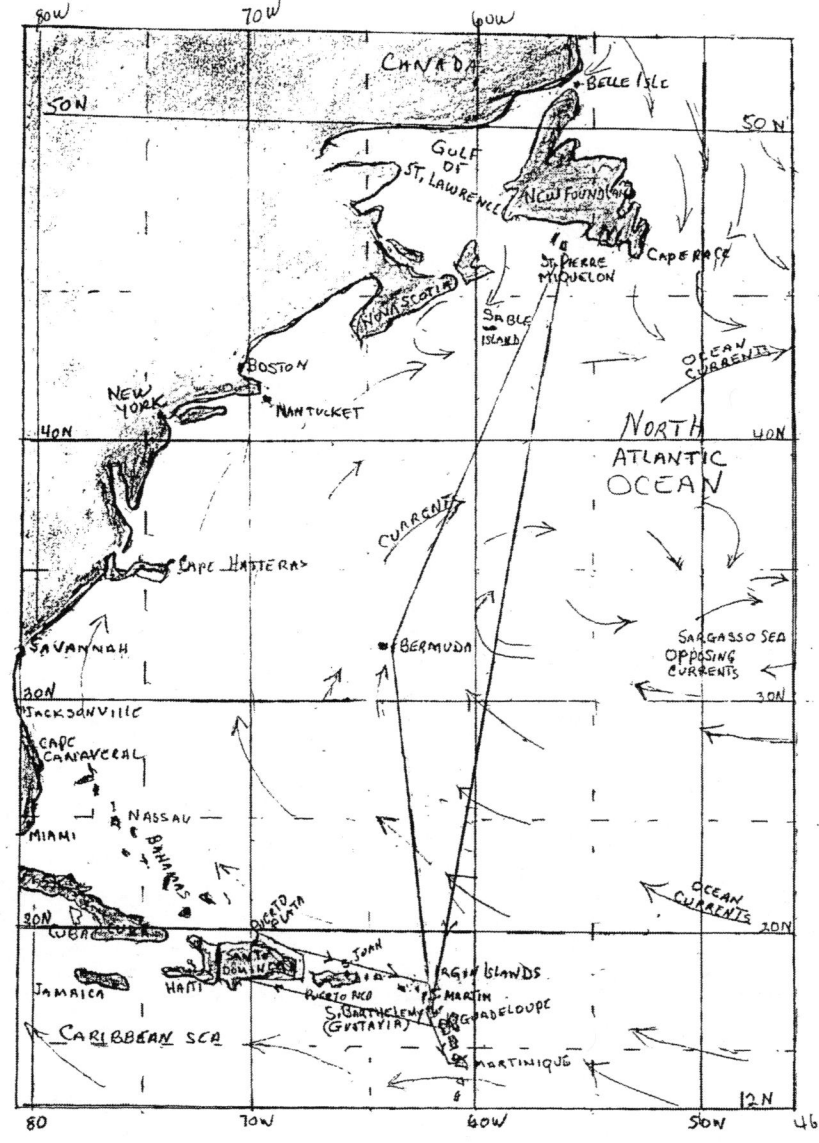

THE WAYWARD BOY
FINDING DISCIPLINE

ACTION
ADVENTURE

VOYAGES ON THE Tall Ship "Putnick"

ISBN 141206508-9